W9-BHZ-366

Dance in Gymnastics

A Guide for Coaches and Gymnasts

Denise Gula

Photographs by Terrence J. Gula

ALLYN AND BACON, INC.

Boston   London   Sydney   Toronto

Library of Congress Cataloging in Publication Data

Gula, Denise, 1949–
   Dance in gymnastics.

   Includes index.
   1. Dancing.   2. Gymnastics.   I. Gula, Terrence J.
II. Title.
GV1595.G78   1986   796.4'1   85-26775
ISBN 0-205-08642-X

Printed in the United States of America

10 9 8 7 6 5 4 3 2 1 90 89 88 87 86 85

to
Michael Sweeney

MICHELE JONES
MODEL FOR *DANCE IN GYMNASTICS*

Michele Jones began gymnastic training in New York, participating in gymnastic competition throughout New York, Pennsylvania, Indiana, and Ohio. In 1976, Michele became the Indiana State Champion on balance beam.

Michele attended both Boston School of Ballet and School of Cleveland Ballet on scholarship and earned the right to compete in the Arts Recognition and Talent Search held in Miami, Florida in 1983, winning a Merit Award in the ballet category. Presently, Michele is a dance major at Butler University in Indianapolis, Indiana.

Contents

Abbreviations

In describing dance movements for the gymnast, the following abbreviations are used throughout the text:

Right	R.
Left	L.
Position	Pos.
Step	Stp.
Cross	X
First	1st
Second	2nd
Third	3rd
Fourth	4th

Where numerical counts are supplied to the description of a particular exercise they refer to the counts or beats in a musical phrase. Where the counts go up to 3 and then begin again with count 1, the beat or pulse implied is that of a waltz. When the written word *and* appears along with the counts, it indicates that a step or movement takes place on the pulse between the beat or between two counts.

Introduction

This book takes the basic principles and techniques of dance and presents them in a manner that is relevant to the gymnast. It is in no way meant to replace the benefits that come from exposure to dance by professional teachers whenever possible. Rather it presents a method of dance that is applicable to the gymnast.

Dance in Gymnastics was born out of personal frustrations experienced while working with gymnasts in competitive gymnastics. Over and over I found myself confronted with two glaring obstacles. The first was to teach the advanced gymnast dance movements that were both appropriate for her skill level and suitable for performance in competition, when she did not have even the most elementary understanding of the basic techniques of dance. The second obstacle was getting and keeping the attention of the gymnast long enough to convince her that understanding the principles of dance was necessary and would not deter her from her main goal and love: gymnastics. I repeatedly found that gymnasts, as well as many coaches, had turned off and tuned out dance because of their personal experience with the often arrogant attitude of dancers who tried to work with the gymnast in the same disciplined fashion and method of instruction that are familiar to the dancer. I felt that there must be a way of presenting dance to the gymnast in terms that she could understand and relate to.

Certainly there are many excellent books available that contain definitions of ballet terminology and technique, but these seem to miss the point for the gymnast, as a certain amount of knowledge of the language of dance is required even to understand their content. In other cases, the dance books just don't go far enough in their explanation to be of value to the gymnast.

Having a background in gymnastics as well as dance, I sympathize with the gymnast's need for dance and recognize the difficulty she has in finding dance training that is applicable to what she is doing gymnastically.

"WHY DO I HAVE TO LEARN HOW TO DANCE?"

The method for training the body and developing the muscles for gymnastics is quite different from that of the dancer. It is often said that it takes ten years of serious study to build a dancer. The task of the gymnast, therefore, is not an easy one, for she must not only be proficient in gymnastics but also possess the skills of a trained dancer. One would not expect a gymnast to execute a round off back handspring-back tuck, for example, without first conditioning the muscles and developing the techniques necessary to achieve such a skill. Nor can one properly execute a dance movement with artistry and grace if the muscles have not first gone through the necessary conditioning and training of basic dance exercise.

While the physical repercussions for the gymnast who attempts to execute a pirouette without benefit of proper technique are insignificant when compared to attempting a gymnastic skill such as a back tuck under the same conditions, it is just as subject to deductions as is the poorly executed tumbling skill. Repeated improper technique in dance movements can also result in serious and chronic injuries, which can jeopardize the future of the gymnast's career. It is advisable, therefore, for the gymnast not only to recognize the basic positions used by the dancer, but also to understand the techniques used in achieving these positions.

The gymnast who has neither training in dance, nor any apparent aptitude for the art, frequently dislikes the floor exercise requirements of competitive gymnastics. Often she is a strong gymnast showing potential in other required areas but falling short in her floor exercise and balance beam performance. This is the gymnast who does not like dance, and why should she? She feels foolish doing it and senses that she looks just as awkward. She feels that it is not relevant to her and she resents being put through the repetitions of basic movements that the dance teacher invariably requires of her.

We all recognize that dance is an important element of gymnastics. But the problem is how to properly expose the gymnast to dance training that she so desperately needs. If she seeks help from a dance school for this training, she meets with several problems. First, the time element. A competing gymnast is already spending most of her available time at the gymnasium working out. Secondly, if she has not previously studied dance, she is enrolled in a beginning class, which is geared to the student with no skills and little or no developed muscular strength. In contrast to the other students, the gymnast is already strong. Her muscles are already developed. Indeed, she may be gymnastically quite advanced and bored with the tedium of a beginning ballet class. Her thoughts may be, "I don't hold onto a barre and point my foot front, side, and back in the middle of my floor routine, so why should I spend hours practicing this?"

Often the gymnast comes away after a year of once-a-week dance classes with nothing concrete that relates dance to her floor routine and, all too often, just plain *hating* dance as well. Frequently, there is little encouragement from the teacher. Regardless of the student's being a gymnast first and in the class only to enhance her gymnastic performance, to the teacher she is a dance student. The teacher sees a student with a muscularly well-developed body and a high level of coordination, and, quite naturally, wants to develop a dancer. This inevitably causes resentment for both parties. And even if the student is fortunate enough to get beyond these problems, it is quite possible that she may never get the help or the training she needs to properly execute that double pirouette. Why? Because in the professional dance school, the student begins with perhaps one or two classes a week. But to be promoted to a more advanced level, where these skills are practiced, generally means attending three, four, or five classes a week. The competing gymnast is obviously not in a position to devote this kind of time and attention to dance. So what happens? She never progresses to the level in her dance training that would teach her how to properly do that pirouette.

One option for the gymnastics school is to import a dance teacher into the school to work with the gymnasts, preferably one with a background and understanding of gymnastics who can relate to the needs of the gymnast. The other alternative is for the coaches personally to become more familiar with the techniques of dance.

It has been my experience that it is possible to develop a program of dance warm-ups and combinations that are both interesting and relevant to the gymnast. If this, along with technical corrections by the coach, are given to each gymnast while she is performing, the entire team will gain the benefits of dance training.

The key is to make the material as interesting and relevant as possible. A carefully planned and well-integrated program can have amazing results. The amount of available time that can be devoted to dance will naturally have to be determined by the coaches when evaluating their own individual work-out schedule. Even the team whose group work-out schedule is limited to three sessions per week will benefit from routinely introducing dance into their schedules. Remember, however, that there are no instant results. The gymnast did not learn to tumble over night. Schools that have a progressive system of classes that feed into the existing competitive team are well advised to begin introducing dance to the beginning students as a normal part of the curriculum. By rotating the dance warm-ups and limiting the practice of dance steps to one particular movement at a time, coaches will find that even twenty minutes a week will be time well spent. Obviously, more than that is recommended for the team with a heavier work-out schedule. It is important to remember that much of the gymnast's progress will have to come from verbal repetition on the part of the coach while the gymnast is performing individually. Their reminders of proper dance technique must follow through into the individual floor and beam performances of the gymnast. It is advisable to work with the entire team on dance combinations and exercises, but the mistake must not be made of shelving technical corrections of the dance movements once the group work has been completed.

In order for the gymnast to become proficient at dance and to add the grace and line that is necessary for her performance of the floor exercise routine, the basic elements of dance technique and the correct use of the body must become automatic. It is advisable, therefore, that she be exposed to some fundamental ballet classes. If these classes are geared to the competing gymnast, all the better, since the goal of a dance school is to train dancers and not gymnasts. If the gymnast can be exposed to dance within the realm of the gymnastic world, then a better understanding of how the techniques of dance relate to the gymnastic performance can be gained. By utilizing the basic principles of ballet technique, the gymnast will be able to develop more control, grace, and fluidity in the dance movements that are required of her.

ACKNOWLEDGMENTS

I wish to express a special thanks to the numerous people who have generously contributed time and effort in the preparation of this book: to both Susan Braig and Jane Fox for their encouragement and critical evaluation of the content of this text; to Mae Fifelski for her review of the material as well as the tedious task of typing the manuscript; and to Barbara Finegan for her long-standing and constant support and encouragement, as well as for her help and suggestions with this text.

1

Ballet:
Body Placement

All ballet movements begin, end, or pass through one of five positions of the feet. To explain how various steps are performed, this book will refer to the placement of the arms and feet by their classical ballet position. Many of the movements described in this book are a component or element of a larger step. For this reason, specific explanations are made of these elements. Remember that the whole movement will always be performed as well as the individual elements that comprise it.

TURN-OUT

Turn-out is particularly difficult for the gymnast because the gymnast is trained to work from a parallel position of the feet and legs. Consequently, when executing dance movements, it is natural to perform these movements from this parallel position. While the parallel position of the feet is frequently used by the modern dancer and also the jazz dancer, it is not an accepted position for classical ballet. To use a parallel position of the feet and legs while executing any ballet step is incorrect. It will destroy the line of the movement and will jeopardize the successful completion of many ballet steps.

Turn-out is the rotation of the leg from the hip socket as well as from the knee and ankle. To accomplish this, the buttock muscles must be tightened together regardless of what action the legs are engaged in. As the buttocks are tightened, the abdominal muscles are pulled upward so that the pelvis is neither tilted back nor tucked forward, providing a straighter position that allows for only the natural curve of the back. At no time should the feet be turned beyond the rotation the gymnast is capable of at the hip. This can place an undue amount of strain on the knees resulting in subsequent injury. To illustrate, stand in ballet 1st position (heels together, feet turned out). Now bend the knees as in plié (plee-ay). In this position the toes should be directly below the knees. If the toes are behind the bent knees, your feet are turned-out beyond the amount of natural turn-out in the hips. Ideally, turn-out in 1st position is 180°, but until the muscles have become sufficiently conditioned to accomplish this, a turn-out of 100° is acceptable. Obviously the amount of turn-out will vary from one person to another.

A well turned-out leg is the normal position for any dance step; it is also aesthetically pleasing to the eye. The sooner this position becomes automatic for the gymnast, the better the performance of the floor routines will become. Not only will it improve the execution of dance steps, but it also will improve balance on such poses as arabesque (ah-ra-besk) or scale. I cannot emphasize enough the importance of turn-out while executing dance movements. The best way to learn the correct use of turn-out and to make it as natural and as automatic for the gymnast as possible is through a traditional ballet warm-up at the barre. I realize that it is difficult for a competitive gymnastic team to find time to devote to extensive study of the dance, but if the coach and the gymnast recognize the need for improved movement skills, the essential techniques of the various dance elements can be incorporated through a carefully planned workout schedule.

Keeping the Connection

The gymnast's awareness of the gluteal muscles and their relationship to the flexors is an important factor in maintaining turn-out while the body is in motion. The correct rotation of the legs at the hip can only be achieved when the pelvis is in proper alignment. When we begin discussing aspects of movement or parts of the body in an independent fashion, we run the risk of separating one part of the body from another. This kind of isolation contributes to choppy and disjointed movement as well as to disjointed technique. Do not overlook that every part of the body has a connection to, and a relationship with, another part of the body.

Turn-out is not achieved in the isolated area of the pelvis. It is not an entity in itself. Turn-out begins in the pelvis, in the hip sockets, and extends out through the legs and up through the torso by engaging and lengthening the surrounding muscles. Awareness of when and how the muscles connect together will hold the body in proper alignment and will give fluidity to the movement. It can also prevent one muscle or group of muscles from over working, thereby allowing the body to move in a more efficient manner and reducing the risk of over development or strain to the muscles.

Table 1.1 *Exercises for Maintaining the "Connection"*

Starting Position	The Exercise	What to Watch
Begin lying on stomach. Arms in reverse "T" pos. Legs together, feet rotated outward. Gluteal muscle contracted.	Lift R. leg up—slow ct. of 4. Lower R. leg—slow ct. of 4. Repeat this 4 times alternating legs. *Variation* Lift R. leg—slow ct. of 4. Leg remains lifted while you lift shoulders, head, and palms of hands—slow ct. of 4. Lower leg and torso together—slow ct. of 4. Repeat this 4 times alternating legs.	1. Maintain well turned-out legs throughout the ex. 2. Do *not* lose contraction of hip opposite from lifting leg. When you can no longer hold the contraction of L. gluteal while lifting R. leg, go no higher. Work to increase the height of the leg while keeping the connection in the opposite hip. 3. Feel the sensation of pulling the leg long and out of the socket as it is lifted by reaching the R. leg out and away from the waist and then up. 4. Feel the contraction in back of waist as the leg begins to lift. *Important* Do not lift head by lifting the chin. Instead, keep the back of the neck long and open the chest while lifting the back of the head.

3

When we contract the buttocks or gluteal muscles, we also feel the connection to the flexors. These are the muscles interlaced with the gluteals and running down the back of the thigh. This connection pulls the pelvis slightly down and back, allowing for a greater rotation in the socket and relieving pressure in the lower back by separating the vertebrae as the torso is extended upward. The connection is working when you see a dent in the side of the leg where it joins the buttocks. This will be just about along the line of the elastic in the leotard.

BODY ALIGNMENT

The position of the body while executing dance steps or poses is very different from that in gymnastics. Much of the time the gymnast is tumbling, she is using an arched back, resulting in an expansion of the rib cage area and frequently a lift in the shoulders. In the execution of dance, the back is allowed only its natural curve, with the stomach muscles pulled in and upward, the ribs closed, and the chest lifted, while the shoulders are pulled gently down and back. Initially this is a very uncomfortable position for the gymnast and one in which she frequently finds it difficult to breathe. However, this position gives her a very strong torso while executing dance movements and a much more pleasing carriage of the body. This is called placement. It is helpful to think of a cinch around the waist and to feel an equal pull of the ribs and the lower back upwards away from this "center," while extending the pelvis down and away from the cinch. By so doing, there is a lengthening of the torso and separating of each vertebrae. This feeling of length and elasticity must extend all the way through to the top of the head by stretching the back of the neck.

This placement is important in controlling turns, particularly when doing a series of turns, or double or triple pirouettes. It will also aid in the execution of the various leaps. In turns, an arched back and expanded rib cage invariably results in a spiral effect, which causes the gymnast to lose her balance. In leaps it results in the loss of control of the torso, which causes a rocking while in the air and a drop in the body upon landing, reminiscent of the action of a whip.

Exception to this placement is necessary when performing a leap specifically requiring an arch, such as an arch jump, stride leap, or split leap, which uses the arch to bring the back foot to the head. Even with these particular movements, though, the gymnast must recover from the leap, bringing the torso back into proper alignment by controlling the rib cage and maintaining an openness to the chest and shoulder area.

There are three schools of classical ballet technique: Russian, Italian (Cecchetti method), and French. While the principles of technique are generally the same among all three schools, the names for some positions and steps may vary slightly. The greatest discrepancy is in the position of the arms. This text will either refer to the position's most commonly used name or identify its alternate names.

THE ARMS

Figures 1.1 through 1.6 show positions of the arms.

The use of the arms in dance is as important as the use of the legs and frequently as difficult. Just as much thought and effort must be given to the technique and carriage of the arms as is applied to the legs. The gymnast often finds it difficult to coordinate the arms with the legs during dance movements. This is a common problem and will improve with practice so long as gentle reminders as to placement of the arms are frequently given. Through constant repetition, the muscles of the body learn what is required of them and less conscious thought is needed. This memory of the muscles is known as kinesthetic memory. As kinesthetic memory develops, the gymnast will no longer be overwhelmed by the placement and technique of dance.

Although the arms remain in the sockets, keeping their connection, they must also feel the opposition or pulling out of and away from the socket. This gives the arms a feeling of weight. The arms must appear calm but exciting, without tension, and never limp or disconnected. In order to achieve the fullest extension of the arms, they must move freely within the sockets.

Figure 1.1 *In the Russian method, this position is named Preparatory, the Checchetti school names it Low Fifth. Notice that the arms are softly rounded and that the elbows do not protrude but shape the arms into a long oval position. Note also that the hands are nicely shaped with the palms facing inward toward each other. A common error here is to allow the palms to face the thighs.*

Figure 1.2   *Russian First position/Cecchetti Middle Fifth. The arms are rounded in front of the lowest part of the rib cage, with the fingers extended toward each other but not touching. Placed in this manner they frame the upper torso. Care must be taken that they do not cover the chest, as this shortens the line of the upper torso. Also notice that the wrist is turned so that the palms face in to the body and that the thumbs are extended and lie close to the index finger.*

Figure 1.3   *Second position arms all schools.*

Regardless of where the arms are placed during a dance movement, they should be felt to extend out from the shoulder blades with the chest lifted, the neck long, and the shoulders square. If, for example, the gymnast is doing a scale with one arm in front and other to the side, the shoulders must remain squarely in place with the back extended upward and the chin lifted. Twisting the shoulder forward with the front arm destroys the line of the torso and the correct placement of the body. This applies to any movement being executed. The timing of the arms in coordination with the dance step is also very important and will vary depending on the type of movement being executed. Therefore, a detailed description of the placement of the arms is included in the description of each individual step.

Following are some general rules for arm positions in classical ballet. The same rules do not necessarily apply to arm movements in jazz or modern dance.

- The fingers of one hand should not touch the fingers of the other hand. Example: 1st position (there should be space between the fingers).

Figure 1.4 *Third position Russian/High Fifth position Cecchetti method. As in Preparatory position, the arms form a long oval position with only a slight break at the wrists. The shoulders are pressed firmly downward and the neck is lengthened, with the arms gracefully framing the face.*

Figure 1.5   *Fourth position (French School).*

- The arms are always smoothly rounded (no pointed elbows). The only exception is in arabesque position.
- When the arms are extended to 2nd position (to the side), the elbows should not go behind the shoulders. This distorts the line of the thoracic area, displacing the torso.
- When the arms are rounded in front of the body (1st position), or over the head in 3rd (high 5th), the palms must face the gymnast.
- The arms must pass through one classical position to arrive in another. Example: If the arms are in a high position over the head (3rd) and going to finish in a low position, they must be lowered down and through 1st position or open out and pass through 2nd position as they travel.

Any movement of the arms in classical dance or ballet is known as Port de bras (pawr duh brah). Although an in depth understanding of Port de bras is not relevant to the gymnast, certain rules of the movement are worth adhering to because incorrect placement of the arms while in classical positions will upset the alignment of the torso and consequently the step being executed.

The movement of the arms adds style and grace to the dance. Any arm movement acts as a punctuation mark. The hands and fingers should be the last part of

Figure 1.6   *High Fourth position (Cecchetti School).*

the arm to arrive in position and should finish each movement with clarity. It is strongly recommended that the theory of movement developed for classical ballet be adhered to strictly. Once there is a thorough understanding of correct line, carriage, and placement of the arms, the gymnast is in a better position to embellish movement or to take liberties with style. Certainly the gymnast has a great deal of freedom even within the classical ballet positions. It is perfectly acceptable to hold the arms to the side, for example, and to keep the elbows straight, with a break or lift at the wrist. Indeed, gymnastics has developed its own style of ballet arms, which is both attractive and appropriate for the type of movement and dancing required in the floor and beam routines. But remember that any style is only icing. It is the interchangeable component that we can substitute with jazz style arms, modern style arms, or the gymnast's own individual style of arms. The essence of movement, the fact that the shoulders do not hunch, the arms are not limp, the fingers do not appear "sticky"—these never change. And above all, the arms should never flail about meaninglessly. There must be a reason for their movement or the position chosen; the gymnast must always control the arms rather than the arms controlling or dominating the movement.

THE SHAPE OF THE HAND

One would not think that the hands could be a source of such enormous problems, but unfortunately the hands on the gymnast run the gamut from limp and lifeless to looking like they've just been pulled out of a jar of jelly. There is not a great deal that can be said about the look or placement of the hands and, to a large extent, this will be a matter of the coach's preference. Some gymnasts seem to have a knack for moving the hands in a graceful, elegant manner; others look as though they just stuck their fingers into an electrical socket. Be that as it may, it is only a problem if you see it as one. If the carriage of the hands draws undue attention, or if the viewer is uncomfortable or distracted by the look of the hands, then they should be worked with. If not, leave well enough alone. Two approaches may be helpful. First, instruct the gymnast to shake the hands rapidly and then completely relax, letting the hands hang freely. They should fall into a position in which the fingers are rounded slightly, with the index finger curved and lifted slightly higher than the others. Instruct the gymnast to extend the fingers while keeping this same formation so that they remain supple, appearing neither bent nor taut. The index finger is lifted and a little higher than the ring finger. The thumb should remain somewhat tucked, so that it is slightly in toward the palm. The second finger is close to the thumb but not touching it. This is the position the dancer uses. Secondly, instruct the gymnast to be aware of the ends of the fingers and to "feel" energy flowing out through the finger tips.

Remember, while the hands are held firmly, they should never become still or stilted in their appearance.

THE FEET

Positions

1st position: The heels are together with the feet turned-out. Knees are facing outward with the buttocks muscles tightly pulled together. The thigh muscles are pulled upward and the insides of the thighs are held tightly together as in a contraction or isometric action. Caution must be taken so that the pelvis is neither tilted backward nor forward; rather, the pelvis should point directly downward in a straight line.

2nd position: The feet are positioned apart at a distance approximately 1½ times the length of your own foot, buttocks muscles are pulled tightly together. The thigh muscles are taut and the inside of the thigh is tensed as if trying to make the inside of one thigh touch the inside of the other.

3rd or 5th position: The feet are turned out with one foot directly in front of the other. The legs are touching and the buttocks muscles are pulled tightly together.

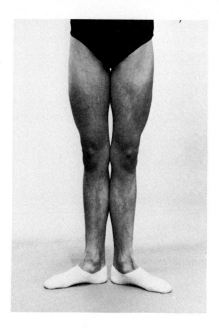

Figure 1.7 *First position.*

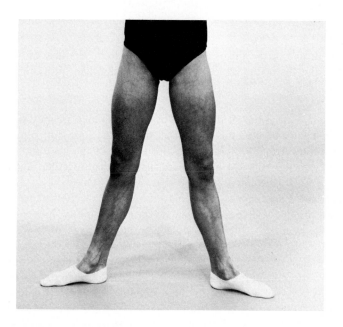

Figure 1.8 *Second position.*

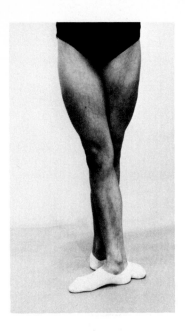

Figure 1.9 *Michele is showing an open position of the feet, with the heel of the forward foot crossed only to the metatarsal of the back foot. This is less strenuous than the purely classical Fifth position and sufficient for the needs of the gymnast.*

Again, the inside of the thighs are squeezed together. The heel of the front foot is crossed to the toe of the back foot. A tight position like this is not recommended for the individual with little turn-out in the hips.

4th position: This is the most difficult of the positions. Care must be taken so that the hips remain square to the front at all times. One foot is in front of the other. The heel of the front foot is in line with the toe of the back foot. Both legs are turned-out and the buttocks muscles are tightly pulled together. Again the pelvis is not tilted back or forward.

The feet are as important a tool to the gymnast as they are to the dancer and deficient technique will certainly increase the risk of injury. Especially in the early stages of the gymnast's training, a close eye must be given to the strengthening of the feet. The key is to observe the foot while in a weight bearing position because if it functions correctly here, it will also function correctly when in motion.

There are three points of balance or support when standing on the foot. These three points take the weight of the body equally. Pressure is firmly applied to the floor from behind, at the heel, and in front through the ball of the foot to the first and fifth toes. The pressure from the small toe helps to prevent rolling inward on

Figure 1.10 *Fourth position.*

the foot and contributing to weak ankles. This triangle of pressure then forms a strong base of support for the arch of the foot and the ankle, as well as allowing the long muscles of the leg to give the balance and stability needed to prevent injury to the ankle. Remember that the foot does not exist independently and that the alignment of the foot to the ankle, the leg, and hips must not be altered. Two important functions of the foot are support and propulsion. The mechanics of propulsion are performed by the toes, particularly the large toe, which provides the push off required for all movements of elevation as well as the finished line to the pointed foot.

EXERCISES FOR STRENGTHENING THE FEET

The following two exercises are helpful in developing strength and flexibility of the foot and encouraging the action needed for propulsion.

Exercise #1

Starting position: Stand with feet parallel, legs straight, abdominal muscles pulled up, gluteal muscles contracted.

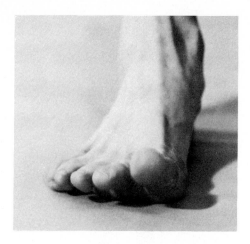

Figure 1.11   *This photo accompanies foot ex. #1 on page 13.*

Exercise: Raise all toes off the floor, keeping heels and metatarsal (ball of the foot) firmly on the floor. Starting with the small toe, press each toe independently into the floor. *Repeat several times. Then repeat exercise in same fashion but with feet turned-out.*

Exercise #2

Starting position: Lying on back, L. leg extended, R. leg raised perpendicular to floor with knee bent. Low back flat to floor.

Exercise:

With R. foot pointed, flex ankle.	2 counts
Pull toes to flex metatarsal.	2 counts
Press ball of foot (metatarsal) to pointed foot; toes remain flexed.	2 counts
Extend toes out, lengthening to full pointed position.	2 counts

Repeat 8–10 times with each leg.

Important:

- Action should take place in a smooth and continuous fashion.
- Pelvis remains flat with abdominals pulled upward.
- Non-working leg remains straight, with the feeling of being pulled out of the hip socket, while maintaining the connection in the buttocks.

As a rule, dance movements should never be executed flat-footed. The foot should remain well pointed until the moment of contact. Begin by extending the leg to the front, turned-out from the hip, so that the knee is facing outward with the foot pointed and the heel lifted. Transfer the weight onto the front leg by touching the toe to the floor, then the ball, and finally the heel. When this is done, the foot is not parallel but turned so that the toes are pointed slightly outward with the heel of the foot facing in. This process is known as "going through the foot." There is *no* exception to this. If the gymnast is doing a dance step of any kind, this is the correct way to step onto the foot.

When leaving the floor as in a jump or leap, this action is exactly reversed. By going through the foot, the body is propelled into the air as the foot pushes the floor away.

Once the whole foot is on the floor, all five toes must be firmly pressed into the floor for balance. Note that in a relevé (rel-a-VAY) position (raised on the ball of the foot), the toes also will be pressed into the floor, a point frequently overlooked. Although the shape and structure of feet vary dramatically from one individual to another, the position of alignment and the muscular action will always remain the same. However, the individual's personal structure must be taken into account. For example, consider the raised position of the foot (relevé) performed by the gymnast with a relatively "square" foot where all five toes are approximately the same in length. This type of foot will have little trouble keeping all of the toes on the floor in relevé and, as a result, will more readily maintain correct alignment of the ankle and turn-out, which will increase the ability to balance.

By contrast, the foot with a very long large toe is less able to press all of the toes into the floor and still maintain proper alignment. One of two problems is likely to occur. Either the foot rolls toward the big toe, making it difficult to hold the connection in the buttocks that maintains the line of the pelvis and results in less consistency when trying to balance, or the foot rolls outward in the effort to pull the little toes to the floor. This strains the ankle. The gymnast with this type of foot may have to lower the height of the relevé and work to lengthen the toes, increasing muscular strength, so that she is able to employ proper technique.

Sickling the pointed foot is another common error. This is seen when the foot is pointed and the leg turned outward, but the ankle and heel of the foot are dropped down toward the floor instead of pressing the ankle up toward the ceiling. It is an unattractive position for the foot because it destroys the line of the leg.

THE HEAD: SPOTTING AND FOCUS

The use of spotting is necessary for any type of turn. This is accomplished by focusing on a point in space before the turn. Observe a point in space slightly above eye level. Leave the focus there as long as possible while the body begins its rotation, then quickly turn the head around to focus at the same point in space before completing the rotation. To illustrate, stand looking at a stationary object directly in line with the focus. Slowly begin to turn the body to the right while still looking at this object over the left shoulder. When the object can no longer be seen, quickly turn the head as far as possible to the right until it is brought back into focus. Continue turning to the right until the body catches up with the head and is facing the object. The use of spotting will greatly improve the control of any turn.

Focus is the action of leading any movement with the eyes, whether it be a change in body direction or a change in arm movement. The use of focus can make a great deal of difference in how the gymnast looks when performing. Without clear focus there can be difficulty regaining composure and finding direction in the routine. This also contributes to the robot-like appearance of some gymnasts while executing dance movements.

Let's consider an example in which the gymnast finished a forward tumbling pass on the diagonal with a front handspring front (tuck) and plans on following this with a leap series to her right. The leap series is:

chassé to the right	step R.L.R.
tour jeté	brush with L., land on L.
back walkover	kick R. leg, land on R. leg
½ turn and chassé	step L.R.L.
split leap	R. leg forward

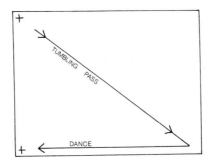

As the gymnast finishes the front tuck, she will be facing away from the floor exercise mat with her focus in this outward direction. Before beginning the chassé to the right, the head should turn so that she focuses in the direction she will be traveling. As she kicks up into the tour jeté, her head should turn so that her focus is now in the direction she has moved from. This happens at the very height of the tour jeté and therefore leads the rotation of the body. The gymnast's focus remains here until she lands. She now does the back walkover and her focus again is in the direction she has traveled from. Before beginning the chassé with the left foot, she should again turn her head to the left so that the focus leads the movement and she is looking in the direction she is traveling. This should be standard procedure for any dance step.

Now let us examime how this works in a pose:

- Begin standing in center of floor mat with the body facing corner 2.
- Pose on L. leg, with R. leg bent and crossed behind L. leg (attitude à terre) and head and eyes focused to corner 2.
- Step back on R. leg and ¼ turn to L. as you step onto the L. leg into a scale position (shoulders are now facing corner 2).

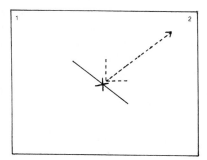 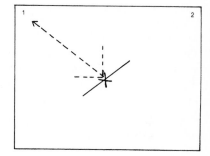

Before her body executes the ¼ turn and as she steps back with the right foot, the gymnast should change her focus from corner 2 to corner 1 to lead the movement. This action of the head will improve her balance of the scale and add clarity and style to the movement.

ARABESQUE

A strong and beautiful arabesque on the beam or the floor is a tremendous asset to the gymnast. Once the gymnast fully understands the mechanics of the arabesque, a high level of success can be achieved in developing the strength and balance required of this position. The arabesque may then be used more extensively by combining it with other movements that lend a greater degree of difficulty to the routines.

Begin with point tendu to the back. This must be performed correctly before lifting the leg into arabesque. Consider first the all important position of the pelvis and abdominal muscles. As the leg is extended to the back, the abdominals must be tightened and pulled upward as though attaching themselves to the bottom of the ribs. The rectus abdominal muscles (see illustration 3.1) control the tilt of the pelvis, thereby controlling the curvature of the lower back as well as pulling down on the ribs. Keep in mind that muscles work in opposition to each other. When the foot is flexed, for example, the calf and back of the leg are stretched. Here, when the abdominals are contracted, the lower part of the spine is flattened. As the leg extends to the back, it reaches down and out, away from the waist. The leg remains well turned-out from the hip but care is taken to keep the hip bone of the working leg pressed forward and the muscles in the back of the waist contracted. The connection in the buttocks is maintained at all times, both in the working leg and in the supporting leg. Practicing the exercise described in Table 1.1 will help strengthen this action.

Now let us look at what the torso is doing. The spine is fully stretched and lengthened away from the pelvis. There is a slight adjustment of the torso diagonally forward. This adjustment makes room for the natural lift in the hip that occurs when the leg is extended to the back. If the adjustment is not made, the spine sinks into the pelvis creating strain in the lumbar region.

This is the correct position of point tendu to the back. Arabesque is simply an extension of this position. As the leg begins its lift, the pelvis will tilt forward, but the gymnast must resist this tilt as much as possible by maintaining a strong upward pull of the abdominals. The higher the leg, the more the pelvis will have to tilt. The torso will also continue to incline forward as the leg lifts, but only to the extent necessary and always maintaining a strong stretch upward and away from the pelvis.

There are essentially four crucial areas to watch for during the arabesque.

Figure 1.12 *First Arabesque (side view). Notice the line of the arms as they extend outward away from the body without distorting the position of the shoulders. The back leg is fully stretched and the spine is extended upward away from the hip of the raised leg.*

1. Make sure that the connection in the buttock of the supporting leg is tightly held as the leg lifts to the arabesque so that the hip does not appear higher than the foot. The tendency is to let this muscle relax as the leg gets higher. Remember to practice the previous mentioned exercise to correct this problem.
2. See that the stomach is well pulled in and lifted during the arabesque.
3. Be sure that the hip bone of the lifted leg is pressed down and forward as much as possible. Do not allow it to twist back, turning away from the supporting leg.
4. Think of the waist as a center line dividing the torso in half. The spine extends forward and upward away from the waist as the leg reaches back and downward away from the waist.

Positions of Arabesque or Scale

The positions of the arabesque are shown in Figures 1.12 through 1.18.

Figure 1.13 *First Arabesque (back view). The shoulder blades are pulled down and the neck is well stretched, lengthening the spine upward and away from the waist.*

Figure 1.14 *Second Arabesque. Here the torso is twisted so that the opposite arm of the supporting leg extends away from the torso. Notice that the shoulders are stretched fully, causing the back arm to be visible from the side view. The forward shoulder is pulled down toward the waist.*

Figure 1.15 *Third Arabesque. In this position the same arm as the supporting leg is elevated. Both shoulders are down and the chest is lifted. Notice that the back of the neck is well stretched.*

Figure 1.16 *Arabesque allongé. In this position the torso is tilted forward more than it is in a normal arabesque position, but the torso and neck are still fully stretched.*

Figure 1.17 *Attitude Devant. Michele's position is lovely here. She shows a nicely stretched attitude position with the foot raised to the height of the working hip, which is carefully pulled down.*

Figure 1.18 *Attitude Derriere. Michele again shows a beautiful line in the upper torso, with the neck extended and the thigh pulled behind the hip of the working leg.*

2

The Language
of the Dance

This chapter presents some of the language of dance. The purpose for defining dance terms here is twofold. First, the terms will be used as descriptive words throughout the book to indicate the manner in which a certain movement may be performed, i.e., in relevé or plié, or in describing the mechanics of a particular dance step. Secondly, these movements or positions are the essence of many dance steps. For example, plié, followed by a brush and a sous-sus in the air, are the components of an assemblé. The finished product will only be as good as the individual elements which comprise the whole movement.

The terms described here do not represent a complete list of the movements traditionally used with a ballet barre but have been chosen for their relevance to movements that are applicable to the gymnast in her floor or beam routines. A more complete listing of dance steps with definitions and teaching instructions is presented in Chapter 4.

PLIÉ

Plié (plee-AY) is a bending of both knees at the same time, or a bending of one knee while the other is in another position. In the best position, the knees or knee remains over the toes. The feet are never turned-out so far that the knee cannot remain directly over the foot, or else undue strain is placed on the knees. The feet, including all five toes, are firmly pressed into the floor.

A plié is necessary to begin and finish any jump or leap and to begin and finish certain types of turns or pirouettes. The movement of plié should be a smooth and continuous action with no jerking or abrupt stop at the bottom of the movement. The bend of the knees is never greater than you are able to achieve while still maintaining the heels firmly into the floor.

The action of a plié should be so smooth as to seemingly appear to melt into the floor. Although the body is being lowered toward the floor by virtue of the bending at the knees, the torso does not sink or drop into the floor. Rather the spine should continue to lengthen by lifting the abdominals and hip bones while feeling the top of the head reach for the ceiling so that there is a counterpull in the torso. Note that the line of the pelvis does not change and that the connection in the buttocks is held. One should not appear to "sit" in the plié but rather to grow up out of the movement. This is extremely important in all movements of elevation so that the flow of upward energy and momentum is not taken down into the floor and stopped before propulsion. On recovery from a movement of elevation, the counter pull in the torso controls and lightens the landing by working to resist the pull of gravity.

Figure 2.1 *Plié (correct). Thighs are pressed back so that the knees are directly over the toes.*

Figure 2.2 *Plié side view (correct).*

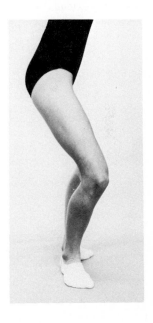

Figure 2.3   *Plié side view (incorrect). Hips are tucked under pressing the knees in front of the toes.*

Figure 2.4   *Plié side view (incorrect). Here the hips are tilted forward so that the rear presses back and the body weight is shifted incorrectly off the feet.*

POINT TENDU

In point tendu (tahn-DEW) the working leg slides from 1st or 5th position to 2nd or 4th position without lifting the toes off the floor. After the toe reaches its extended position, it returns to the 1st or 5th position by reversing the process and sliding the foot on the floor as the leg closes.

This is an exercise to strengthen the foot and instep and is also the beginning and ending position of any brushing movement. The hips remain square, legs straight and well turned-out, with the muscles on the inside of the thigh taut. This movement is an undercurve. The energy extends down through the working leg to the foot, pressing into the floor, and continues outward as the leg opens to the extended position and the ankle lifts to a stretched foot. Pressure from the foot is applied into the floor as it extends out and also as it returns to the initial position. As this is accomplished, the instep is fully stretched and the toes are exercised, lengthening them as much as possible.

When the leg moves to an open position in back, the connection of the buttock to the flexors must be carefully maintained. (The flexors are those muscles which control the rotation of the hip joint.) This is accomplished by keeping the outward rotation of the leg in the hip socket while firmly pressing the buttocks down as the leg extends, and at the same time lengthening the torso upward away

Figure 2.5 *Point tendu front. Both legs are well turned out with a fully stretched foot.*

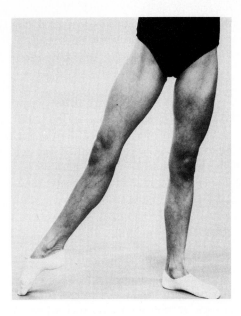

Figure 2.6 *Point tendu side. Both legs are well turned out from the hip so that the knees face out in opposite directions.*

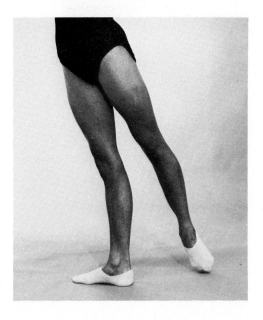

Figure 2.7 *Point tendu to the back.*

from the back of the waist. Visualize an imaginary rod running from the waist through the hip to the ankle as the leg reaches to the back.

DÉGAGÉ

Dégagé (day-ga-SHAY) is simply a continuation of the point tendu with the foot lifting off the floor at the end of the extended position. It is, however, a much quicker action than point tendu. The foot must be seen to brush firmly in and away from the floor by first pushing down into the floor to give greater impetus to the brush. This is the beginning movement of many steps of elevation, such as assemblé.

COUPÉ

Coupé (koo-PAY) refers to the area of the leg between the ankle and the base of the calf. Coupé position is when one foot is placed at the ankle of the standing foot, either in front or back, so that the foot is pointed and the knee of the raised leg is bent and turned outward.

Figure 2.8 *Coupé position front. In this position be sure that the knee of the working leg is pressed back and the ankle pressed forward.*

Figure 2.9 *Coupé back. In this position the heel of the foot is in contact with the support leg while the toes are pressed outward so that they do not touch the supporting leg. Turnout is held securely in the hips, and the knee of the working leg is pressed back.*

PASSÉ

Passé (pa-SAY) is an auxiliary movement in which one foot slides up the front or back of the supporting leg and passes the knee as it moves into some other position. The knee of the working leg remains well turned out. The toes are the last part of the foot to leave the floor as the knee lifts.

RETIRÉ

Retiré (ruh-tee-RAY) is raising the thigh so that it is well turned out and the toe is in line with and touching the knee of the supporting leg either in front or in back.

DÉVELOPPÉ

Développé (dayv-law-PAY) is the action of drawing the leg up the side of the supporting leg to the knee (passé) and extending it to the front, side, or back. Through-

Figure 2.10 *Retiré correct.*

Figure 2.11 *Retiré incorrect. Here Michele has allowed her working foot to rest against the supporting leg. This results in a sicled foot and a knee that is too far forward.*

out the movement the hips remain level and square to the front. When the développé is to the front, the foot and ankle will lead the extension as the knee and thigh resist by pressing back and away from the extension. Once the leg is extended, the knee of the lifted leg will face outward away from the body. Be sure that the connection in the buttock is maintained. When the développé is to the side, keep the working hip pulled well down and the knee pressed back as far as the turn-out will allow. As the foot extends it will be slightly in front of the working knee and the hip bone will remain square to the front. Be particularly careful that the hip bone on the side of the working leg does not press back as the leg extends to the side. The height of the knee in attitude position determines how high the leg will be lifted to the side. The foot will describe an undercurve as it swings away from the standing knee, under the thigh, and up to the height of the working knee. The leg may be higher than the beginning height of the working knee and thigh by lifting the leg further at the end of the extension, but it may not be lower than the already established height. In other words, do not allow the knee and thigh to drop as the foot extends outward. If a lower height of the leg is desired, then the foot must begin to développé sooner or before the foot reaches the knee of the supporting leg.

Figure 2.12 and 2.12a *Attitude développé front. Notice that the height of the knee is established while in the attitude position. The working leg extends out from this height so that the knee remains in the same place during the extension. If the leg is to be held at a lower level, then the attitude before the extension must also be lowered.*

Figure 2.13 and 2.13a   *Attitude développé side. Knee height of attitude is same as the knee height of extended leg.*

Figure 2.14 and 2.14a   *Développé back. Michele has intentionally shown the position just before the attitude is reached. Notice that the thigh and knee of the working leg must be pressed back as far as possible before extending the leg and taking the torso forward. This prevents the hip from coming up and the knee from dipping down, an error that is very common in extensions to the back.*

The développé to the back is the most difficult. The hip bone of the working leg must remain pulled forward as much as possible as the working leg rotates in the socket and extends to the back. As the leg is extending, the thigh should be lifted so that it is on the same plane as the foot and not dropped below. Be sure that the leg extends directly behind the center of the back. As the leg extends to the back, a strong contraction of the muscles at the back of the waist should be felt and held firmly throughout the extension. The torso must be seen to lift still further and press very slightly forward to make room for the leg to move back and to prevent the lower spine from "sitting" into the working hip. This will both restrict the range of the working leg and increase tension to this area.

Regardless of the direction of the développé, the movement should be continuous, drawing the energy up with the foot and extending out to the appropriate position. This is both an undercurve and an upward movement, so there must be an abdominal lift and an extension of the torso as the leg lifts. When the leg is extended to the front or side, the abdominal lift is particularly important because it is this pulling in and up and the tightening of the gluteal muscles of the supporting leg that are the key to being able to hold the leg in the extended position.

RELEVÉ

Relevé (ruhl-VAY) refers to rising onto the ball of the foot or feet in any position. In relevé be sure that all five toes are pressed into the floor and that the ankle is in a straight line with the leg.

Figure 2.15 *Relevé correct.*

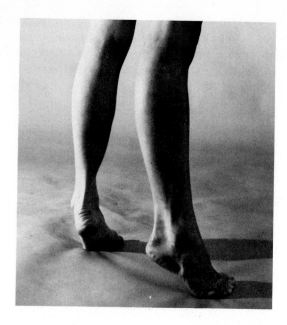

Figure 2.15a *Relevé incorrect. Ankles rotated too far back.*

ROND DE JAMBE

Rond de jambe (rawn-duh-ZHAMB) is a circular movement of the leg in which the working leg moves in a clockwise or counter clockwise direction. The working leg may draw the half circle with the foot on the floor or in the air. All movement comes from the rotation in the socket at the hip of the working leg. The supporting side is well lifted and the connection in the buttock muscles maintained. Here again we have a great deal of support for the working leg coming from the strength of the standing leg and the strong upward pull of the abdominals.

When the leg is lifted in the air, you must be particularly concerned with the placement of the hips as the leg rotates from the front to the side position. The side position will be only as far as the turn-out allows. In other words, the leg may go as far to the side as is possible while keeping the hip bones in line with each other and the buttocks of the working leg pulled down. Once this position is reached, the rotation in the socket must begin to carry the leg to the backward position. Remember that the torso will move slightly forward to allow for the rotation. The height of the leg must be maintained as the leg rotates and moves to the back. The muscles at the back of the waist contract firmly as the leg is carried from the side to the back position.

SAUTÉ

Sauté (soh-TAY) indicates that the movement is to be done as a jump or spring into the air. In sauté pirouette, for example, the gymnast springs into the air on the rotation instead of lifting to a straight leg.

ATTITUDE

Attitude (ah-tee-TEWD) is a position in which the body is supported on one leg while the other is lifted to the back, forward, or to the side with a flexed knee. The supporting leg may be straight, flexed, or in relevé. When the leg is lifted to the front, the knee is pressed out and downward and the foot and ankle are lifted as high as possible. To the back, the knee is bent at a 90° angle and is well turned-out so that it is even with the foot. Remember that in all positions where the leg is to the back, the torso must achieve a greater lift through the body and press slightly forward to make room for the leg.

GRAND BATTEMENT

Grand battement (grahn bat-MAHN) is the action of brushing the working leg into the air so that it is raised from the hip, then lowering it again, closing into the supporting leg. This movement may be taken forward, side, or back. The leg is turned out from the hip. The working leg slides from the closed position along the floor until the foot is fully stretched; it then continues its upward lift into the air, reaching maximum height before returning to the closed position. The action of the leg is seen in one smooth, continuous, sweeping movement. The torso must extend upward with the brush of the leg by a strong lift of the abdominal muscles.

If the leg is brushed to the side, particular care must be taken that the working hip remains pulled down as the leg lifts. When the leg is properly turned-out, the knee of the working leg will face up toward the ceiling. When the grand battement is to the back, there must be a slight adjustment of the torso up and forward so that there is room in the hip socket for the leg to be lifted without jamming the lower spine. However, the adjustment is very slight and barely noticeable. The torso should never drop away from the brushing leg and the hip should remain down to the back. The lift of the leg is initiated by lengthening the working leg down and then out and away from the waist before allowing the leg to lift into the air.

Do not allow the leg to lift from the hip when executing grand battement to the back; this shortens the line of the leg, jams the lower spine, and results in generally poor placement. Here it is particularly difficult to maintain the connection in the supporting leg. The tendency is to drop the pelvis forward in an effort to kick the leg up. This is not correct and practicing the lift in this manner will never develop the muscular control required for proper execution of the arabesque or scale position.

With the leg brushed to the front, the impetus is from the inward and upward pull of the abdominals, and the elevated leg must be seen to crease at the socket. This is accomplished when the hip bone maintains its opposing pull against the forward brush of the leg. As this is done, the crease is secured further by the wrapping of the buttocks muscles maintaining turn-out. Do not allow the pelvis to tuck or rotate under as the leg brushes to the front.

Whether the battement is to the front, side, or back, there must be a strong downward brush into the floor before releasing out and up; this will give impetus to the thrust of the leg. The supporting heel should be felt to continue the strong pull into the floor firmly anchoring the supporting leg away from the working leg.

SOUS-SUS

Sous-sus (soo-SEW) is a relevé in 5th position which may travel forward, back, or to the side. The legs are drawn tightly together with the heels pressed forward so that the front foot completely covers the back foot. Sous-sus begins in plié and springs to the relevé position.

PROMENADE

Promenade (prawn-NAD) is a pivot turn. The heel of the supporting leg lifts slightly and presses forward or back to turn the body on the ball of the foot. The heel presses backward when the rotation is outward (away from the supporting leg); the heel presses forward to rotate the body when the pivot is inward (toward the supporting leg). The working leg may be in any position, and the supporting leg is generally straight with the knee well pulled up. This movement is not difficult so long as the turn-out is well maintained from the hips and the torso held firmly in place with no sideways or twisting movement at the waist. The body must be seen to turn in one solid unit.

PENCHÉ

Penché (pahn-SHAY) means to lean or incline and is generally used in connection with an arabesque. The body leans forward with the head low and the leg reaching to its highest point. Ideally this is a standing split position. However, the torso may only incline as far as the stretch and strength of the arabesque allows. In this way the relationship of the upper back to the arabesque is maintained as the body leans

Figure 2.16 *Arabesque Penché.*

forward. When the leg has been lifted to the maximum height, the torso may not drop any lower. The movement is always initiated by the lifting of the arabesque leg and never by the lowering of the torso.

ATTITUDE À TERRE

Attitude à terre (ah tehr) describes a position in which the gymnast stands on one leg with the other leg bent as in attitude, but the toe is touching the floor behind

Figure 2.17 *Attitude à terre.*

the supporting leg. Closed attitude is when the foot is touching the back of the supporting foot. Open attitude à terre is when the foot is moved backwards about 10 or 12 inches away from the supporting foot. This position is commonly used as a pose or a beginning position of a movement.

3

The Elements

CIRCULAR MOVEMENT: A THEORY IN DESIGN

The body and its range of motion is very consistent. The torso can move forward, backward, and laterally. The legs and arms are capable of a full circular and spherical range of motion by virtue of their ball and socket attachment. The range of movement of knees and the elbows is more limited as hinges, but a hinge also permits a circular motion as the muscles contract at right angles. The body's complete motion is developed from movement patterns that fit this spherical design.

Dance movement also fits this circular design, turning or pivoting on an axis or moving through space on the crest of an undercurve or overcurve. For example, you will recall that the leg brushed down into the floor, to gather energy and impetus to carry the body up into a leap. When this theory of circular movement with its curves is taken into consideration, the step benefits from a fluidity and continuity that would otherwise be lacking. And the body may take advantage of its fullest range of motion from the previous movement, through the connecting step, into the following movement. Even changes in direction become smoother and less abrupt when undercurves or overcurves in the movement patterns are identified and completed before going on to the next move or step.

Moving the body in space creates energy around the body that can help or hinder the movement. It is the task of the gymnast to move the body so that the physical laws help to carry the movement, controlling and directing this energy.

When moving in circular motion, as in a turn or pirouette, the body rotates around an imaginary axis. Movement of the body in larger circles involves centrifugal force (that which impels an object toward the outside of a center of rotation) and centripetal force (that which pulls inward toward the center of rotation) and controls this energy. Rounding the corner on a bicycle and leaning inward too far to compensate for this force causes the bike to tip over. When the gymnast moves from a static position, energy must be gathered to overcome the physical law of inertia. Once the energy is gathered and directed in complement to the surrounding space, momentum will carry the body and do the work. What all of this means is that movement must be in harmony with itself as well as with the physical space around it.

The very fact that movement takes place means that the space around the object creating movement is disturbed, changed, or affected in some way. If we identify and understand the pattern of a specific movement, we are better equipped to control the space around that movement. If the movement is explosive, for example, then the arms and legs gather the energy within the body and send it out from its center to the very tips of the fingers and toes—like a fish that explodes out of the water, splashing in all directions. When the body turns, as in a pirouette, the arms open at the beginning of the turn, pushing the air away and then drawing it in again to create a vacuum for the body to turn within. As the body moves in space, the arms collect the energy about the body, controlling, taking it with the movement, and then releasing it out again.

Always the hands and the feet maintain a relationship with the space around the body. Like a life support, they gather energy in and release it out from the center of the body.

BREATHING

Proper breathing is essential for the sustaining power needed by the gymnast. Obviously, stamina is an important factor for any athlete and good breathing habits contribute to this vitality, but the value of proper breathing techniques is not limited to providing stamina. Breathing exercises introduced early in the training of the gymnast will strengthen abdominal muscles, increase the co-ordination and quality of certain movements, improve elevation, serve as a means of "pacing" the floor exercise, and become a successful tool to calm and prepare the gymnast for performance. The importance of breathing technique is often overlooked by both dancers and gymnasts.

To understand proper breathing, we must go beyond the idea of just breathing through the mouth or even that of deep abdominal (diaphragmatical) breathing. We must do more than simply remind the gymnast to "breath." The gymnast must be trained to breathe properly through the use of breathing exercises and then instructed on the timing of the inhalation that most benefits the movement. For example, to execute a split leap, the gymnast should inhale deeply on the preparing step, hold the breath while in the air, and exhale on the landing. The inhalation of air fills the lungs with oxygen, giving the movement lightness; the pulling upwards of the abdominals during the inward breath helps to lift the body; the exhalation softens the landing. It is not possible to breath evenly or in a relaxed rhythmic fashion during execution of difficult movements or exercise. Our bodies force us to breath in uneven intervals, to take in the additional oxygen needed because of exertion. Through proper, controlled breathing, the gymnast can pace herself, saving breath while combining several movements before exhalation.

The excitement experienced by the gymnast during competition is an emotional reaction that can affect the rate of breathing. Breathing may become tense, resulting in shortness of breath during performance, reducing endurance, and contributing to the general nervousness which detracts from the presentation. The breathing exercises in this chapter are intended to teach the gymnast to focus on her "center," meaning the area between the bottom of the rib cage and the hip bones. Controlled breathing conserves energy and supplies the body with the needed fresh oxygen required by the gymnast to successfully complete a routine. Focusing on the "center" helps to eliminate outward distractions and produces a sense of calm, increasing concentration and enhancing performance.

Timing the Inhalation

1. Movements of elevation: Breathe in, pulling abdominals upward with the breath as the foot pushes the floor away. Hold the breath while the body is in the air, exhale as the leg or legs land in a demi-plié.

2. Rising into the relevé: To balance in a relevé position or to control a pirouette, inhale as the body moves from the plié onto the ball of the foot. Hold the breath as balance is maintained. Exhale as the position is released. If turning, hold the breath until the rotation is completed and exhale as the turn is finished.

3. Movements of transfer such as chassé: Filling the lungs with air lightens the body at the moment of transfer. Consequently, the working leg is more able to move against the force of gravity as it propels the body forward.

BREATHING EXERCISES

The following three exercises are helpful in facilitating lower abdominal breathing and readying the body for movement.

Exercise #1

Starting position: Begin standing with arms at sides, feet parallel, shoulders relaxed and neck lengthened, focus out, buttocks muscles contracted.

Exercise:

Breathe deeply through the nose filling the lungs with air and raising arms to sides until palms touch over head.	slow ct. of 4
Hold position.	slow ct. of 4
Breathe out through the mouth while lowering arms forward and down, palms in.	slow ct. of 4
On last count, sharply contract abdominal muscles forcing all of the air out of lungs.	ct. 5

Exercise #2

Starting position: Begin standing with hands on hips, feet parallel, shoulders relaxed and neck lengthened, focus out, buttocks muscles contracted.

Exercise:

Breathe deeply through nose.	
Holding breath, bend torso to the **R.**	hold ct. of 2
Lift chest and bend back (do not bend knees).	hold ct. of 2
Bend torso to left.	hold ct. of 2
Bend forward from waist.	hold ct. of 2
Breathe out sharply through mouth, contracting abdominal muscles.	slow ct. of 4
Roll up through spine to starting position, breathing deeply through nose.	
Repeat exercise 4 times.	

Exercise #3

Starting position: Begin standing with arms at sides, feet parallel, shoulders relaxed and neck lengthened, focus out, buttocks muscles contracted.

Exercise:

Breathe in deeply through the nose.	slow ct. of 4
Holding breath and maintaining contraction in buttocks, roll down through the spine beginning with chin on chest.	

Sharply contract abdominals, forcing air out.
Roll back up through the spine,   slow ct. of 4
   breathing deeply through the nose.
Repeat exercise 4 times.

To achieve the desired results from the preceding exercises, there should be no excessive tension in the body and proper emphasis must be kept on the breathing. Instruct the gymnast to pull the abdominals in and up during the inhalation.

- Feel a lengthening of the spine through the neck and out of the pelvis.
- Visualize the air being drawn up from the abdomen along the inside of the spine to the top of the head.
- Feel the front and back of the rib cage lift equally out of the pelvis.

The following exercises are for increasing abdominal strength and coordinating of the breathing with the movement.

Exercise #1

Starting position: Begin lying on back, knees bent, and feet flat. Place arms beside the body. Rotate pelvis under so that lower back is flat to floor.

Exercise:

1. Inhale through the nose to a slow count of 4. As you begin the breath, lift the chin and shoulders slightly off the floor and reach the left hand across the right knee, rolling up through the spine but maintaining the pelvis flat on the floor. Breathe out through the mouth to a slow count of 4, rolling down through the spine and keeping the shoulders relaxed.
2. Repeat the exercise, rolling up to the left to a slow count of 4 and down for 4.
3. Repeat to the center, rolling straight up, crossing the arms at the wrist, lengthening the spine out of pelvis and along the floor as you breathe in for 4 counts.

Do 4 sets of this exercise.
   Important:

- Focus eyes on stomach as you roll up. Do not allow the abdominal muscles to push outward as this defeats the purpose of the exercise. Instead, feel the muscles scoop in and lift upward along the spine.
- Be sure to use all four counts to breathe in during the lift and all four counts breathing out as you roll down.

Exercise #2

Starting position: Begin lying on back, arms in reverse "T" position, with legs open and extended to sides in wide second.

Exercise:

1. Lift the right leg by pressing the low back flat and drawing abdominal muscles up as you breathe in to count of 4. (Don't roll the pelvis; keep the buttocks tight.)
2. Maintaining flat shoulders, extend the R. hip up toward ceiling as you begin to cross the R. leg as far to the left as possible, exhaling to count of 4 as this is done.
3. Return leg to horizontal pos. by pushing R. hip out and away from the waist while breathing in to count of 4.
4. Maintaining flat pelvis, lower R. leg to original position while breathing out to slow ct. of 4.

Alternate legs, repeating exercise 4 times.

WEIGHT TRANSFER

When transferring from one foot to another, the entire body must move onto the new supporting leg while maintaining correct alignment and placement of the torso. Accurate transfer of weight is essential because the working leg becomes the supporting leg. Appreciation of this will keep the dance movements smooth and flowing and enable the gymnast to maintain the necessary speed and balance.

Independent analysis of weight transfer for various movements will be necessary since the timing and impetus of the transfer may vary depending on the specific movement as well as its purpose within the routine. For example, if the movement performed is assemblé, and it is to be done in place, the weight will remain over the supporting leg. As the working leg glides outward, at the moment that the toe is about to leave the floor, the supporting leg will press into the floor to propel the body upward. At the height of the jump, the working (brushing) leg will land in the same spot in which the jump began. The weight remains centered over this spot throughout the jump.

If, however, the assemblé is to travel, the movement begins in the same manner but the working (brushing) leg will give greater impetus and the toes will leave the floor just before the spring into the air. In this case, the spring will be both upward and toward the direction indicated by the working leg. The weight is re-centered over both legs as they come together before landing. Here the weight transfer has taken place in the air, enabling the gymnast to finish the movement with a controlled landing. Without the correct weight transfer, the body would be behind the legs and the landing would be off balance.

In any jump or leap the center line of balance, and consequently the weight of the torso or the transfer of weight, will:

- Remain in place and centered over the legs.
- Direct the movement by anticipating the line to be followed.
- Make the weight transfer or adjustment at the height of the movement so that the torso is correctly centered on the landing.

Correct Weight Transfer for the Five Types of Jumps

1. Springing from one leg and landing on same leg: No transfer of weight is required because the body is already centered over the supporting leg. All that is necessary is for the gymnast to feel the fullest extension of the torso, which means controlling the muscles involved in placement so that the body does not wobble while in the air. Maintain this control during the landing. If the spring is to travel in some direction, as in a cabriole, then the head and torso should be directed toward the line of travel and give impetus to the movement. In a fouetté, where there is a change in direction while in the air, the same rule applies but the gymnast must give stronger impetus from the supporting leg and arms so that the change of alignment can take place swiftly at the height of the spring. Note that the alignment remains the same here, and that there is no transfer of weight.

2. Spring from two feet to two feet: The weight of the body remains centered over both feet from the beginning of the spring to the landing. Impetus will come from a strong and equal push into and out of the floor by both feet. If the spring is to travel, the head and torso will direct the line of travel. Examples of two feet to two feet jumps are changement (shahnzh-MAHNT), entrechat quatre (ahn-truh SHAH ka-truh), royale (rwah-yal), and soubresaut (soo-bruh-soh).

3. Spring from two feet to one foot: The body is centered over two feet. Impetus comes from both feet and the transfer of weight comes at the height of the movement so that the body is centered over the supporting leg on the landing. Examples of two feet to one foot jumps are sissone open (see-sawn) and sissone closed.

4. From one foot to two feet: If the movement does not travel, the weight will remain over the supporting leg from the beginning to the end of the jump. If the movement travels, the transfer of weight will take place in the air and adjust over both feet as the legs join in preparation for the landing. Examples of one foot to two feet jumps are assemblé (ash-sahn-blay), assemblé battu (ba-tew), and brisé (bree-zay).

5. From one foot to the other: On the take off, the weight is centered over the supporting or pushing leg. The weight is stabilized between the two legs and the body is centered. Depending on the type of leap executed, the body will then either transfer over the landing leg, beginning the adjustment at the height of the leap, or it will remain where it is and the landing leg will move under the torso as the body descends. Examples of leaps from one foot to the other are all types of jetés, split leaps, stride leaps, and glissade (glee-SAD).

BALANCE

Balance is achieved by aligning the body over its base of support while stabilizing the torso. Stabilization is accomplished by lengthening the spine, retracting and elongating the neck (keeping the head in line with the back), and by engaging the abdominal muscles to keep the pelvis properly aligned. When the balance is over two feet, the base is broad and the center of gravity is between the two feet. If the feet are opened away from each other, as in 2nd or 4th position, balance is easier because the torso remains centered between the two feet. When the balance is over one foot, the center of gravity must be shifted over the standing leg so that the torso remains aligned to its base. The difficulty here is primarily in the hip area. Care must be taken so that as the center line of gravity is adjusted, the torso does not lean or incline over its single-footed base; rather, the hip bones should remain on the same plane. The hip bones must remain level at all times during any adjustment of the torso so that proper alignment is assured.

Balance is complicated further when any body part is moved away from the center line of gravity. Try to imagine a pole running down the center of the body from the top of the head through the back and spine. Imagine that the limbs of the body are attached to this pole, which is the center line of gravity. If one leg is moved to the side, there must be an adjustment of another body part to maintain balance. The torso must make a slight shift over the supporting leg. Balance is further stabilized by feeling the lengthening of the torso and control of the pelvis and waist. Whenever one part of the body is moved away from the center of gravity, there must be an adjustment made in alignment to compensate. If the position taken to balance is on relevé, the base for support is further diminished and the amount of strength, concentration, and control required is increased; no muscle needed can be lax. Elongation of the spine must be greater to compensate for the smaller base of support. Control of pelvis, waist, and turn-out must be strengthened and any error in the adjustment or alignment of the torso over the center of gravity will make the balance quite difficult, if not impossible. There can be no weak link and wobbly ankles are often the culprit. Pressing the heels forward while keeping all five toes firmly into the floor will stabilize the ankles.

4

Pirouettes

A pirouette (peer-wet) is a complete turn of the body on one foot, either to the inside or to the outside. An inside turn is made inward toward the supporting leg. An outside turn is made away from the supporting leg.

Although knowledge of classical ballet technique is necessary for a gymnast to perform well in a floor routine, one is not restricted to classical turns. Exposure to both modern and jazz dance will broaden one's understanding of the types of turns not found in the ballet class. If the principles for executing a turn are applied, the gymnast can create any number of turns that are visually appealing.

Regardless of the type of turn executed, or whether the back is straight or arched, the shoulders must remain directly in line with the hips, and the hips must be over the supporting foot. If the turn is done with a straight body, the shoulders will remain directly over the hips throughout the rotation. If it is an arched turn, such as an arabesque turn, it will be impossible for the shoulders to stay over the hips. But they will still be in line with the hips. If the turn was stopped at any point, the shoulders would be square with the hips and not twisted. This is accomplished by keeping the abdominal muscles pulled in and upward and keeping the rib cage under control without expansion. Remember, the connection is kept in the buttocks as the knees bend for the preparation of the turn as well as during the lift and throughout the rotation. Once these principles are integrated into the turn, any type or style may be created.

Coordinating the controlled intake of breath with the turn will increase the stability of any type of pirouette. The breath begins as the gymnast rises from out of the preparation or bent knee position. The breath should be timed so that it continues throughout the turn, is held briefly at the end of the turn, and is exhaled as the working foot returns to the floor. The holding of the breath at the end of the turn will give the pirouette a feeling of suspension. Apart from the stability this gives to the turn, the suspension also improves the quality of the turn, giving it a finished or polished look. The points gained in competition for performing a difficult double or triple turn are hardly worth the effort if the gymnast receives deductions for whirling or spinning out of control.

Too frequently the gymnast allows the pirouette to become a source of difficulty, becoming intimidated by the turn. When this happens, the gymnast is no longer in control—the turn is—and we have what I like to refer to as "spin and pray." There is nothing quite so beautiful and impressive as seeing that slight pause or suspension at the very end of the rotation, exhibiting the utmost skill and complete control of the turn. Controlled abdominal breathing helps to calm the body and allows the gymnast to focus attention and find her center before the turn. In this way, the turn or pirouette is controlled from within.

Very little force is needed to rotate the body. One does not need to throw the arms harder to send the body around. In fact, if the body is properly placed and correct technique is employed, one and even two rotations in some types of turns is quite possible without the use of the arms at all. The purpose of the arms in a turn is primarily for balance; it is the abdominal lift and the legs that are responsible for turning the body.

When doing turns, keep the following rules in mind:

1. The gymnast must spot.
2. The hips must remain directly over the supporting foot while turning.
3. The shoulders must remain directly over or in line with the hips.
4. The supporting leg and foot are kept turned-out during the entire rotation of the body.
5. The upper body must be controlled with proper alignment while executing the turn.
6. The breathing must be controlled and coordinated with the rotation.
7. The waist must be firmly held.
8. The gymnast must keep the connection in the buttocks.

If any of these rules are broken, the gymnast will sacrifice the turn and have an end product which she cannot count on. A solid turn is not the result of luck. It can only be accomplished by the application of sound ballet technique.

If the gymnast is losing control while turning, close observation should enable the coach to identify the problem. For example, if the gymnast is consistently falling out of the turn, check if the line of the hips is out of alignment with the supporting leg just before or during the turn. Remember that the hips must remain directly over the supporting leg throughout the rotation. If the turn ends with the upper body twisted beyond the hips, check to make sure that the turn is not being initiated by the upper body. The shoulders must remain over the hips throughout the turn, and the foot begins its pivot immediately so that the leg remains turned-out from the beginning to the end of the turn.

USE OF THE ARMS

During the execution of almost any turn, the gymnast is greatly aided by her arms. The gymnast should begin with the arms in ballet 4th position (one arm rounded in front of the body and the other arm extended to the side). When turning to the left, the left arm will be rounded in front of the body. As the rotation begins, the forward arm should open slightly in a controlled fashion to the side of the body, while the second arm should immediately close to the first arm. This procedure should be followed regardless of the position chosen for the arms while executing the turn. If the arms are to be held rounded and over the head during the turn, the gymnast proceeds in the same manner, but as the arms come together into 1st position, the hand and elbow stop just in front of the shoulder so that one is not thrown off the center line of balance. The timing of this action should be coordinated with the turn so that the movement of the first arm precedes the rotation while the movement of the second arm is simultaneous with the rotation. Remember that very little force from the arms is required to accomplish the turn.

USE OF THE LEGS

A turn may be executed from either a straight or bent knee. If the gymnast is doing a turn on a straight leg, such as an arabesque turn, the leg that is to become the turning leg should first be extended with the foot pointed. The gymnast will then step as far out onto the leg as possible, being careful not to step flat-footed but high onto the ball of the foot, with the knee remaining well pulled up. If the turn is from a bent knee, the knee should be straightened as the first arm opens to the side and at the beginning of the rotation. This is where the inhalation of breath will occur.

USE OF THE TORSO

Maintaining the gap between the pelvis and the rib cage is critical. The gymnast must always feel the abdominals pulling upward, separating the rib cage from the hip bones. At the same time, the lowest part of the back must feel open as it lifts out of the pelvis from behind. In this way, the distance between the upper part of the body and the pelvis remains the same all around the body. Remember that while this is accomplished, the rib cage is held securely and the spine is lengthened through the back of the neck to the head. At no time during this lifting should the rib cage open apart in an effort to move away from the hip bones.

As the body begins its rotation, there is no twist in the waist. The abdominal muscles must be engaged so that the torso makes its rotation as though the gymnast were wearing a corset.

The spine is capable of a great deal of movement and it is the movement of the spinal column in relationship to the abdominal muscles that must be controlled during the turn. Lateral flexion (right or left movement of the shoulders toward the hips) and rotary movement of the spine in the horizontal plane are the two movements that cause the most problems in a pirouette. It is essential for the abdominal muscle group to be engaged during the turn so that the torso is held in correct alignment.

Rectus Abdominal Muscle

This muscle runs laterally and pulls down the rib cage. It also controls the tilt of the pelvis and consequently the curve of the lower spine. By pulling up on the pelvis in front, it relieves pressure in the lower back.

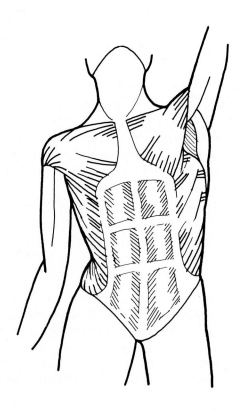

Oblique Externus and Internus Abdominal Muscles

These muscles control the twist of the rib cage, right or left, away from the pelvis. When all of these muscles are engaged, the torso, the pelvis, and the rib cage will maintain correct placement, helping to secure the successful completion of the turn.

EXAMPLES OF TURNS

Attitude Turns

The turn is executed on one leg. The free leg is lifted to 90° and bent slightly with the foot pointed and the knee turned-out. The free leg may be held in front of the body, to the side, or to the back.

Pirouette

The turn is executed on one leg, while the free leg is bent and the toe is at the knee or ankle. The free leg may be either turned-out or in parallel.

Soutenu Turns

Bend the left leg or knee; at the same time, point the right leg to the side. The right toe remains on the floor as you draw it across the left. Rise onto the balls of both feet while you pivot the body so that you are half way around. (The right foot is still in front of the body.) Continue the rotation so that you are facing front again. The left foot is now in front of the right.

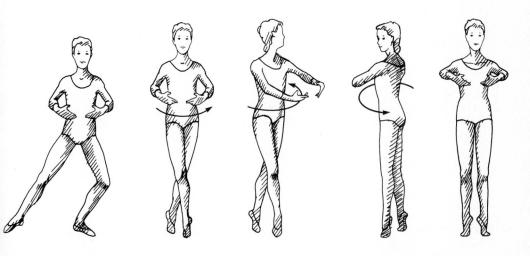

Detourné

Detourné (day-toor-NAY) is a very nice, small turn particularly useful on the beam. It may be done as either a full or half turn. As a half turn, begin with the right foot pointed to the back. Very simply, make one half turn toward the back foot so that at the completion of the turn the back leg becomes the front leg. This may be done as a pivot or raised fully on the ball of the foot. It may be done à terre (toe on the floor), en l'air (leg raised in the air), with the leg straight, or in attitude.

As a full turn, detourné is performed in the same manner, except that at the end of the first half turn when the back leg becomes the front leg, you continue turning in the same direction, halfway around, keeping the new forward leg to your front as you turn. A simple variation is to precede the half or full turn with a small rond de jambe. Plié on the left leg and point the right leg to the front. Rond de jambe with the right leg to the back, staying in plié. As the leg arrives in back, relevé onto the supporting leg and turn to the right into the detourné turn. This could easily become a 1½ turn.

Piqué

Piqué (pee-KAY), is a turn performed by stepping directly onto the ball of the extended leg with the raised leg in retiré (foot at the knee), coupé (ankle) front or back, attitude, or arabesque. The turn may be inside or outside. Piqué means pricked or pricking, so the spring onto the ball of the foot should be a sharp staccato movement, with the free leg moving immediately into the desired position.

Renversé

Renversé (Rahn-vehr-SAY) literally means "upset" or "reversed." The body bends from the waist during the turn so that normal balance and placement is upset while

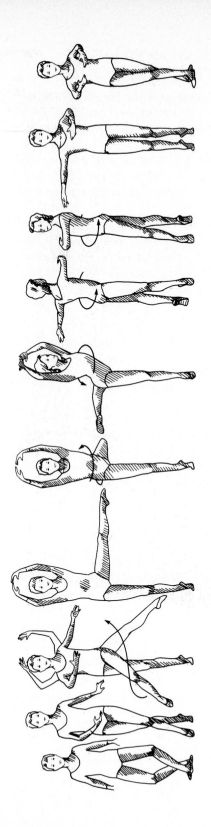

still maintaining one's equilibrium. The movement generally begins by "cutting" one foot under the other. Start with the left foot pointed back, close the left foot to the right, cutting under with the left so that it replaces the right. The right foot is then thrown forward. From here, the right leg lifts into the air to execute a rond de jambe to the right, which finishes in attitude back with the supporting leg bent. Now close the right leg behind the left and execute a pas de bourre turn finishing forward. (Cross the right behind the left, step ½ turn to right on the left, and finish by stepping on the right to face front.)

As this is done, the torso will bend forcefully from the waist, first to the left and then to the back while the pas de bourre is performed. Both arms will swing down in front of the body and to the right, continuing directly side and lateral, then smoothly overhead and to the left side lateral position. The left arm stays in the side position as the right arm opens away from it to the side right position. Remember:

- As the R. leg moves up in front, arms down R.
- As the R. leg moves side, arms move up.
- As the torso bends L., arms move L. but still overhead.
- As the turn finishes, arms move side L. and then R. Arm opens side R.

Note that there should be a sustained holding of the attitude back position before going on. Also, the tilt left of the upper body will slightly precede the lowering of the leg, so that for a moment we see a beautiful arch and tilt of the upper back, arms, and lifted leg.

By making some minor changes, any of these previously described turns may be altered to give the gymnast an entirely new turn.

- The turn may be executed in relevé (ball of the foot) while the supporting leg remains straight.
- The gymnast may execute the turn with the supporting leg bent.
- The rotation of the turn may be in the air. (Begin the preparation with the supporting leg bent and straighten the knee as you propel into the air.)

Changing the arm position may also add variety to the turns:

3rd position arms: The arms are rounded over the head while turning.

1st position arms: The arms are rounded and held in front of the body while turning.

Oblique arms: The arms are held in a V position.

2nd position arms: Arms open to the side of the body while turning. (Note that the hands will remain slightly in front of the shoulders.)

If the turn is to be a double, consider placing the arms in one position for the first rotation and another position for the second rotation. For example, arms in 1st position on the first rotation, lifting to 3rd position. The arms may also be crossed at the wrists and held in front of the body. Or one arm may be stretched to the ceiling with the second arm held down and along the side of the body (with slight side arch in the body toward the lower arm).

EXAMPLES OF TURNS IN THE AIR

Tour en l'air (toor ahn lehr)

Technically this jumping turn reverses the feet while in the air and may be performed as a single or double turn. The gymnast generally does this turn without the change in feet.

The beginning position is 3rd (right foot in front of left). The knees are bent. Springing sharply into the air, pushing the floor away, straightening the legs, and pointing the toes, the body begins rotating to the right. The change of the leg takes place while in the air so that the feet land in 3rd position but with the left leg in front. If the turn is to the right, the left arm is brought in sharply to meet the right arm, giving impetus to the turn.

Emboîté turns (ahn-bwah-TAY)

This is a quick jumping turn, alternating from one foot to the other. The jumps are not high, but do travel and have a light, elastic quality. The take off is from two feet to one, landing on the right foot, lifting the left foot at the front of the ankle and completing a ½ turn to the right. Immediately spring into the air, pushing off the ground with the right foot. Still turning to the right, but landing on the left leg with the right foot at the left ankle, execute another ½ turn. Two springs equal one full turn or rotation.

Saut de basque (soh duh bask)

Begin by stepping down onto the right foot to the side position. Turning to the right, immediately brush the left foot in the same direction as the first step. As this is done, push the floor away with the right foot so that the brushing action propels the torso into the air. Continue turning to the right (one full rotation) and land on the left foot, with the right foot at the ankle of the left (coupé) and the right knee bent.

Some Variations

1. Tour en l'air may finish on one foot with the other at the ankle.
2. Tour en l'air may finish on one knee.
3. Tour en l'air to arabesque turning to the R. finish on the L. in plié with the R. leg moving immediately to arabesque.
4. Embôité may be combined with the tour. Two embôités springing onto the R. foot (½ turn to R.) and then onto the L. foot (½ turn to R.). Bring R. foot together with L. and execute one full turn to the R.
5. Embôité may be combined with and used as a preparation to an acrobatic move or some type of leap. For example, two embôités (one rotation): spring onto R., then L. Step down onto R. and brush L. into side leap.

TURNS USED IN A SERIES

A series of turns is any combination of turns executed one after another while traveling in a direction, or more than one turn repeated, such as chainé turns.

Chainé Turns (sheh-NAY)

A chainé turn (sheh-NAY) is executed alternately on one foot, moving forward in a single direction. When turning to the right, the first half turn will be on the right foot, the second half turn will be on the left foot.

To practice chainé turns, stand sideways on a line. Prepare for the turn by beginning with the left foot on the line, the right foot pointed in front of you, and the head turned to your right over your shoulder looking in the direction of the line. Swing the right leg to your side and step on the line. Now continue turning to your right, bringing the left leg in front. Immediately bring the right foot around to your right and step again onto the line, allowing the feet to pivot (½ turn). Continue in this fashion staying on the balls of the feet, knees straight, and legs well turned-out. Remember that the shoulders must remain directly over the hips throughout the rotation.

The arms: While executing chainé turns, the arms may be held rounded in front of the body (1st position). They can cross at the wrist and gradually move upward to the ceiling in a stretched position. Or they can even be held straight out to the side of the body in 2nd position.

COMBINING TURNS TO CREATE A SERIES

Example #1

Attitude turn to the right: Stand on the L. leg, with the R. leg pointed to the front. Begin by stepping onto the R. leg and swining the L. leg into front attitude position as you turn right. One full turn.

Outside pirouette: Step onto the L. leg and turn to the right with the R. foot at the ankle. One full turn.

Right turn in the air: Immediately place the R. foot beside the L. and bend knees. Jump into the air turning to your right. Land on the L. foot, bringing the R. to the side of the ankle of the L. foot. One full rotation. As the right turn in the air is completed, one may go into an acrobatic movement such as a walkover or immediately drop down onto the R. knee and begin floor work.

  In this example, the gymnast is performing three full turns, so the head will spot or focus front three times.

Example #2

Soutenu pirouette: Soutenu turns may also be useful in combining two turns to add more difficulty or interest to the turn.

  Execute soutenu turn to the left, crossing the R. foot in front of L. One full turn.

  Immediately upon completing the first rotation of the body, transfer weight onto the R. foot. Pick up the L. foot and place it at the front of the R. knee as you continue turning in the same direction. Two full rotations.

Example #3

Rond de jambe en l'air to attitude back: Step forward onto the L. leg and brush the R. leg off the ground to the front, then to the side, finishing back in attitude. Arms move to 1st position when leg is forward. Open to 2nd position as the leg moves side, finishing in 4th position (L. arm to the side, R. arm over head). Remember to adjust the torso slightly forward as the leg moves to the back.

Promenade in attitude ½ turn to the right: Immediately apply backward pressure to the thigh of the R. leg and pivot on the ball of the L. foot. Be sure to keep buttocks muscles tight. Arms remain in previous position.

Arabesque turn to the right: Lower the R. leg from attitude, stepping down behind the L. leg. Legs may momentarily be seen in 4th position plié. Transfer the weight of the body onto the R. leg, pivoting to the right (½ turn), and immediately lifting the L. leg into arabesque. As this is done, the R. arm will lower across the body and lift into 1st position arabesque arms. As the body passes through the transitionary 4th position plié and straightens into the arabesque, the gymnast will make one full turn to the right on the R. leg. Two full turns.

Example #4

Arabesque soutenu: One full turn in arabesque on relevé to the right. (L. leg is in the air, lifted in back of the body.) At the end of the first rotation, plié on the supporting leg and immediately swing the L. leg to the side and in front of the body as you relevé and execute the soutenu turn to the right. Two full turns.

OTHER USES OF TURNS IN A FLOOR ROUTINE

As a connecting step into an acrobatic move: Double pirouette into a front walkover or tinsica. This is a superior move.

As a skill by itself: Execute a double arabesque turn ending in plié on the supporting leg and stop the turn without losing balance. Also a superior move.

In a leap passage: Turns may be used to introduce and end a leap pass, or as part of a combination that includes a leap. For example chaîné, chaîné, step right leap left, step right tour jeté with left, step right pirouette.

As a method for getting to the floor: Double or single pirouette, kneeling down to the floor on the free leg immediately following the pirouette. Or double pirouette followed by an extension of the free leg to the back, finishing with a chest fall.

FINAL THOUGHTS ON TURNS

All pirouettes may be executed as an inside or outside turn; that is, turning to the right on the left leg and away from the left leg, or turning to the right on the right leg. Notice that in each case, the turn is to the right, but with an inside turn, the turn is made toward the supporting leg. With an outside turn, the turn is made away from the supporting leg.

Almost all turns can be executed as a single, double, or triple turn. In each case, spotting is used. The method for spotting remains the same, except when executing a 1½ or a 2½ turn. When this type of turn is desired, the gymnast must change the spot. This is accomplished by completing the half turn before beginning to spot. In other words, look in the direction that the turn begins, immediately continue the focus to the opposite direction (where the turn will finish), and then spot that direction as the front while executing the full turn. For example, turn 1½ times on the right foot with the left foot at the right ankle. Step on the right foot looking to the right. Turn halfway around, keeping the focus over the right shoulder. This is now your front. Execute one full turn leaving the focus over the left shoulder to spot as the body continues turning to the right.

5

Leaps

It is not necessary to describe the various types of leaps, since the gymnast is already very familiar with her options in this area. Instead, the discussion will be limited to the proper execution of a leap.

USE OF THE LEGS

The standard leap must begin with a sufficient amount of bend from the take-off leg and enough power behind the kicking leg to achieve proper elevation. Remember to maintain the connection at the buttocks of the take-off leg; also maintain the left of the abdominals and control of the waistline while kicking. When the leap does not have enough height, is generally weak in appearance, or has a seesawing effect, the problem lies with either the take-off leg or the pelvic placement. There must be no hesitation between the kicking of the forward leg and the push off of the back leg, with the action of the kick taking place only an instant before the push-off. The legs must act as a spring in both the take-off and the landing of the leap. If the gymnast bends the knees in preparation for the leap but stops the action momentarily before the push-off, the gymnast defeats the purpose of this spring-board action, interrupts momentum, and sacrifices elevation. Poor pelvic placement or lack of abdominal lift may cause the back leg to droop in a split leap. A simple reminder to keep the hip bones lifted up will often correct the pelvic placement and give the leap that stretched, even, split that is desired.

The gymnast should not land flat footed. Rather, she should land "through" the foot (toe, ball, heel), allowing the supporting leg to bend. The heel must get to the floor and remain there until recovering from the leap. The supporting leg will absorb the shock of the landing if there is sufficient bend of the knee to prevent jarring of the body. A firm heel to the floor will also protect the ankle and achilles from serious strains and injuries.

USE OF THE TORSO

As the gymnast travels forward in space during the leap, so must the torso. When landing, the body weight will be slightly forward over the supporting leg. It should never be behind the supporting leg. On take-off from the leap, the chest should lift diagonally up and forward, while keeping the shoulders down and square. Many gymnasts pull the shoulders up with their arms as they leap into the air, which destroys the line of the body. Again it is noted that the gymnast must not allow the pelvis to rotate backward, away from the kicking leg, as this interferes with correct body alignment. This is prevented by lifting the abdominals as the leg is kicked (keeping the hip bones lifted) and by maintaining the connection in the buttocks. Remember, too, that the ribs must not expand or this will result in an arched back with the weight behind the supporting leg upon landing. Landing in this fashion will cause the body to take all of the strain of recovery in the lower back, which is the weakest point in the spine. Continued stress to this area can eventually cause injury to the lower back. Of course, if the leap requires an arch in the back, then the gymnast must recover from the arch upon landing.

BREATHING

Breathe in on the preparation step. Hold the breath in on take-off and while in flight. Exhale with the bending of the support leg after landing.

USE OF THE ARMS

In a leap, the arms may be held in the oblique position (as in a "V"), 3rd position (over the head and rounded), vertical, or in arabesque (opposite the legs, with one arm stretched forward and the other extended to the side). Remember, when the arms are in arabesque position, the shoulders must remain square to the front.

Path of Travel

1. Oblique: Arms move from low side position directly to high oblique. Impulse at the elbow first and then allow the forearm and hands to lead the movement.

2. 3rd position: Begin arms in side position, then scoop arms down on preparation step, and lift through 1st position on take off.

3. Arabesque: From side position, arms scoop down on preparation step, lift to 1st position (rounded in front of body), and then open directly to arabesque position (one arm forward, one side) on take-off. The arms may also be lifted directly to the arabesque position from the low position, eliminating the passage through 1st position. Be careful that the side position is to the side and not behind the shoulder and in back.

THE STRIDE LEAP VERSUS THE SPLIT LEAP

If the leap is to have a light, airy quality, and the landing position of the leap is to be held and balanced, then the gymnast executes a grand jeté. If the leap is meant to travel quickly through the air, the gymnast executes the more modern and athletic leap known as split leap.

The *International Gymnastics Federation Code of Points* indicates that the difference between the split leap and the stride leap is that in the latter the legs do not reach a flat, split position in the air. In dance, this is not necessarily the case and the grand jeté, or what would be referred to as a stride leap, may or may not reach the full split while in the air. In dance, the difference between the two leaps is rather in their style and execution. The type of leap performed will be determined by the style of the movement in the routine, the music, and the quality presented. An even more important determining factor may be what is required of the gymnast upon landing. In some cases the gymnast may find that to accurately perform the required landing in a routine, she must execute the stride leap, achieving a flat split in the air, i.e., the grand jeté.

In the purely classical grand jeté, the movement describes a half circle with the brushing leg. Impetus for the take-off is given as the supporting leg presses firmly into the floor and the working leg brushes out. At the moment of flight, the torso will curve very slightly backwards so that the head and weight of the body are behind the jump. At the height of the leap, the legs are equally stretched out from each other into a split, and both front and back legs are at equal distance from the floor, while the torso is well stretched and directly between the legs. The body then begins to travel downwards toward the landing position. The toes of the forward leg follow the curve indicated at the beginning of the leap. The body then lands in an arabesque, the pose having been anticipated before the landing. Once in this position, the gymnast may choose to move out of the arabesque immediately or remain posed for a moment before going on. The line of the arabesque is already formed and the transfer of weight has taken place prior to the landing.

When executing a split leap, which is used more often by the gymnast, the torso and head are directed straight forward, indicating the line of travel, while simultaneously pushing off the floor and immediately opening both legs to the split position. The weight remains more or less centered throughout the leap and the legs endeavor to remain at equal height from the floor as the body travels in its line of direction. In a beam routine, for example, if the gymnast is expected to hold the arabesque pose upon landing from the leap, certainly the execution of a classical grand jeté would be managed more easily than the traditional split leap. Holding an arabesque from the split leap is not impossible but is more difficult. To balance, the body must simultaneously stretch out and up from the landing leg into the arabesque line while descending into the plié. The quality of the split leap is forceful and darting; the gymnast appears to "cut" through the air with forward speed and momentum that makes holding a landing position quite difficult. While the split leap requires more strength and energy to perform, the classical grand jeté is more difficult to coordinate.

EXERCISES FOR IMPROVING THE QUALITY OF LEAPS

#1. *Leg Extension Side*

The purpose is to develop understanding, thrust of weight transfer, and the ability to rapidly extend feet and legs completely from a bent or plié position.

Starting position: Begin by stand in wide 2nd position plié. Legs and feet are well turned-out, knees firmly pressed back. Arms are extended to the side. Abdominals are well pulled up, hip bones lifted to control the line of the pelvis.

Exercise:

1. Without tilting the hips, strongly shift the torso horizontally over the L. leg keeping it bent.
2. Simultaneously release the R. leg completely, extending the knee and ankle to the side, so that there is a straight line from the hip to the toe.
3. The leg is not high but the abdominals will feel a strong pull and the connection in the buttocks is maintained to prevent any backward tilt of the pelvis. The leg is extended as far from the body as possible with a strong thrust. The position is then momentarily held or suspended before shifting the body back to its starting position.

Alternately practice the movement using as strong a thrust as possible with a momentary suspension of the leg each time.

#2. *Leg Extensions Forward and Back*

Starting position: Begin with the legs in a wide 4th position. Perform in the same manner as in the previous exercise, but moving forward and back instead of side-to-side. Throughout the exercise be sure that the spine and neck are lengthened and extended upward.

Exercise:

1. Begin with the forward shift but allow the leg to take a small step to the front. As this is accomplished, the abdominals are lifted and care is taken to keep the hip bone of the extended leg pressed forward.
2. Simultaneously shift the weight forward over the supporting leg and immediately extend the opposite leg behind and just off the ground.
3. Reverse the process, stepping to the back. Be sure to crease at the hip socket of the lifted leg, exerting an opposing pull away from the lengthening of the leg.

SWITCH LEG TO A SPLIT LEAP

Special consideration must be given to the switch leg split leap because its take-off is unlike the leaps previously described. Please be aware that this leap, though particularly beautiful and impressive, is simply a trick and no more difficult to perform than any other leap. The trick is to propel the body straight upwards—not forward—with a strong push from the take-off leg. If the gymnast attempts to switch the legs while propeling forward one of two situations is likely to arise. Either she will not have enough time in the air to successfully execute the switch of the legs, and we will see two very poor stride positions. Or the momentum and speed of the forward thrust during take-off will cause the gymnast to nose dive as the legs attempt to make the switch. If instead, the gymnast thinks of taking both the brushing leg and the body straight *up* and not *out* during the take-off, she will be able to execute the switching of the legs quite successfully. This is also true of the switch leg split leap variation in which the forward brushing leg passes through retiré and developés to the back as the legs switch positions. (Switching leg is straight, bent, and then straight.)

6

The Steps and Their Definitions

TEACHING AND USING THE DANCE MOVEMENTS

Assemblé

Assemblé (ah-sahn-BLAY) is a step of elevation. Beginning in plié with the right foot in back, brush the back foot well into the floor and out to the side. As the working leg leaves the floor, strongly push off the floor with the supporting leg so that the leg is well stretched and the toes pointed. Both feet come together to land simultaneously in 5th position plié.

Mechanics:

1. In the plié position, feel the torso erect. Do not "sit" or hinge at the hip but keep the connection in the buttocks.
2. The supporting leg remains in plié with the heel firmly into the floor until the working leg has reached its fullest extension on the floor. The body weight remains firmly over the supporting leg during this extension.
3. The push-off of the supporting leg will occur simultaneously with the brush away from the floor of the working leg.
4. On the spring upward, the abdominals will continue to lift, taking the hip bones up.

5. At the moment of descent there must be further muscular tension in the buttocks to soften the landing.

Variations:

1. Beginning with the R. foot back, brushing side and closing with R. foot front (over).
2. Beginning with the R. foot front, brushing side and closing with the R. foot back (under).
3. Standing with R. foot front, brushing forward and traveling to the front, closing with R. foot front.
4. Starting with the R. foot back, brushing backward and traveling back.
5. Turning. Turns must be preceded with a preparatory step of some kind. Brush the R. foot to the side. As the legs begin to come together in the air with the R. foot in front, rotate the body to the left, landing with the R. foot forward after one full rotation. The crossing of the R. foot in front will give impetus to the rotation. The inner thighs must be held firmly together. Arms begin extended to the side; then move to preparatory position on the step and bring the arms to 1st and then 3rd position as the body lifts and rotates. Remember that the torso must remain fully stretched and the shoulders completely over the hips so that the landing from the turn is centered and in control.
6. With a beat. Beginning with R. foot back, brush R. leg to side and push off the floor with L. The legs come together in the air with the R. foot in front, but quickly switch the legs so that the L. leg is in front on the landing. The beat may also be back-to-front so that the R. leg finishes front. Note that all beats are executed correctly when the legs are crossed at the uppermost part of the inner thighs. The beat is not of the ankles but of the legs.
7. Assemblé soutenu. Begin with R. foot back. Demi plié and slide R. leg side to point tendue. Immediately pull the R. leg back to the L., springing up into 5th position relevé or sous-sus position. Please note that this is not two separate movements but one continuous action down into the plié and up to the sous-sus. Accent is up.

All assemblés may be large or small. The height of the movement is determined by the height of the brushing leg.

Balancé

Balancé (ba-lahn-SAY) is a rocking movement consisting of three steps. Begin with the right foot in back, 5th position. Plié and brush the right foot to 2nd position. Spring lightly onto the right foot into plié and cross the left foot behind the right, inclining the head and the body to the right. Step up onto the ball of the left foot behind the right, so that the weight of the body is taken off the right foot. Step down onto the right foot, lifting the left to coupé back. The next balance would be to the left.

The arms may swing freely from side-to-side with the movement or lift up and over the movement (side left, up to 3rd position, and to side right). The movement is executed to the count of three:

count 1. Spring onto the R. foot.
count 2. Step up on the ball of the L. foot.
count 3. Fall forward onto the R. in plié

Variations:

1. Traveling forward or back.
2. Traveling side-to-side.
3. Turning inward. Take a large side step to the right with the R. foot. Step behind the R. with the L. foot and execute a turn (½ to ¼) to your left as you take the step. Continue turning slightly to your left as you transfer the weight forward onto the R. foot. (You have now completed one-half of the rotation.) Step to the side with the L. foot; transfer the weight onto the R. foot stepping behind the L. Finish facing forward by continuing to turn to the L. as you transfer the weight again onto the L. foot. It takes two balances to complete one rotation.
4. The turn may also be executed to the right, turning outward. Step to the side with the R. foot. Cross L. behind R. Step onto the R. and execute a ¼ turn to the right. As this is done, take the next step to your left, crossing the R. further behind the L., and turning ¼ further to the right. Finish facing forward as the final step is taken on the L. foot. It takes two balances to complete one rotation.

Ballonné

To execute the ballonné (ba-law-NAY), begin in 5th position, right foot front, plié on the left and brush the right forcefully forward. As this is done, push off the ground with the left foot, jumping forward. (Both legs are momentarily stretched into the air, the left being extended directly under the torso and the right extended forward at a $45°$ angle.) As the left foot descends to the plié position, the right simultaneously bends at the knee to cross the foot in front of the left ankle (coupé). From this position the movement may be repeated before moving on to something else.

An interesting line can be created by twisting the torso at the waist in opposition to the brushing leg and extending the arms into a forward diagonal position, complementing the beating leg. If the right leg is brushing forward, the left shoulder would be twisted forward, right shoulder back. The right arm is lifted in back and the torso tilted slightly forward at the waist as the left arm reaches toward the beating foot.

Mechanics:

1. Both legs are fully stretched out of the hips and extended to the toes while in the air.
2. Both legs remain well turned-out while in the air as the body moves forward in space.
3. Connection in the buttocks is maintained upon landing and both knees are bent with the R. thigh pressed back.
4. Accent is on the landing. Brush on the "and," land on count 1.

Ballonné means "bounced" or "ball-like," and the movement should be light with a clear cutting of the foot to coupé position.

Figure 6.1 *Position shown is both the beginning and the ending position of the Ballonné.*

Variations:

1. Turning—The springing foot is the center or axis of a circle, with the brushing leg extending out and in as the body rotates. Two or three ballonés make one rotation.
2. As a preparation for another movement—One ballonné (R. foot to L. ankle; then step forward onto the R. foot to move to the next movement. Example: Step L., ballonné R., step R., split leap L.
3. Performed in a series as two or three ballonnés traveling forward on the beam. Note that there would be no step between each ballonné, the movement coming each time from the coupé. Impetus for the spring is from the plié of the supporting leg.
4. Performed by alternating legs as in a skip. Step L. and ballonné with R. foot to coupé front. Step down on R. and ballooné with the L. foot to coupé front.

Ballotté

Ballotté means "tossed" and is a somewhat more athletic movement transferring the weight from one foot to the other with the torso swinging back and forward. The move requires considerable balance. Begin in 5th position with the right foot front. Bend the knees and spring strongly into the air. Immediately draw both feet up to the torso by bending the knees and keeping the legs well turned-out. (The feet and legs appear to be in a small diamond shape.) As the body descends, extend the left leg under the torso to land in plié; simultaneously, extend or "toss" the right leg forward to a 90° height while lifting the torso to incline slightly backward. The head and focus are turned to the left and the left arm is rounded in front of the body (1st position), while the right arm is extended side to 2nd position. From this position, sharply spring back up into the air, again flexing the knees so that the left foot is drawn up under the torso, and the right foot has been pulled in to meet it. (Again the diamond position.) Immediately pass through and out of this diamond shape to extend the left leg behind in arabesque as you land in plié on the right leg while lifting in the torso to incline slightly forward and away from the back leg. The head and focus remain to the left and the arms remain in original position. (Left arm rounded in front to 1st position and the right extended to the side in 2nd position.)

Mechanics:

1. The knees and thighs remain well turned-out and the toes pointed.
2. There must be a very strong abdominal pull upwards to lift the knees into the diamond shape.
3. The extending leg must arrive at its fully stretched position of 90° before springing upward again.
4. The torso is inclined forward and back by a strong abdominal lift and controlled tilt of the torso so the body doesn't appear to collapse or bounce on each landing.
5. Both feet must be clearly seen in the diamond position before the appropriate leg extends. The lift into the air is on the "and," with the extension of the working leg and the landing of the supporting leg on the count.

Variations:

1. Execute only the first half of the ballotté. (R. foot extends diagonally forward to the R., landing on the L.) As the second half is commenced, leave the focus as is, but sharply bring the right arm to 1st position, turning the torso ¼ to the left so that the second leg extends diagonally forward to the left instead of to the back.
2. Perform in same manner but add the back extension. Begin in 5th position with R. foot front. Ballotté and extend the R. leg forward. Turn ¼ to the left as you ballotté and extend the L. leg forward. Remain facing the same direction and ballotté, extending the R. leg back. Your body will incline slightly up and back on the first side, up and back on the 2nd side, and slightly forward on the 3rd phase of the movement.

This might be an interesting movement for an experienced gymnast to combine with a back attitude turn. From the 3rd phase of the movement, the right leg is extended back and the left leg is in plié. Immediately lift up to a straight left leg, opening the arms to the side, and bending the right leg to attitude as you turn on the left leg to the right.

Brisé

The brisé (bree-ZAY) movement is best thought of as an assemblé travelled with a

beat. Brush the right leg forward and off the ground at 45°. Spring into the air with the left leg and bring it to meet the right leg. (Both legs are straight, with the right leg crossed in front of the left.) Immediately change the legs while in the air so that the left calf comes in front of the right with a beat. The landing is in plié on both feet, with the left leg in front (5th position).

Mechanics:

1. The landing of the legs is simultaneous and finishes in plié.
2. Both legs are extended and straight in the air with the back leg coming to meet the front leg on the upward swing.
3. The switch or beat of the legs will take place at the height of the movement so that the opposite leg is in front as the body begins to descend.

Variations

1. Travelling forward and brushing the R. leg to the front, the torso will incline slightly back, drawing the abdomen up and turning the head and focus to the left away from the brushing leg.
2. To the side; the body will incline slightly in the direction of travel with the focus toward the brushing leg and the leading arm rounded to 1st position, with the second arm extended to the side and slightly lifted.

Cabriole

The cabriole (ka-bree-AWL) is a step of elevation. The working leg is thrust strongly into the air; the underneath leg or pushing leg follows and beats against the first leg, sending it higher into the air. The landing is then made on the underneath leg. Begin by stepping onto the left leg, bending the knee, and bringing the torso and body weight forward over this leg. The arms will move from 2nd position down to the preparatory position. As the weight is transferred over the left leg, strongly swing the right leg forward and up to a height of 90°; at the same time lift the arms through 1st position, opening the right arm to the side and the left arm over the head while bending the torso back. Immediately jump from the left foot, swinging the leg forward and up to the right, so that the thighs and calves are touching. This action forces the right leg still higher. The left leg then returns to the floor landing in plié. The right leg is held momentarily before it returns to the floor.

Mechanics:

1. The legs maintain an extended and well turned-out position throughout the movement.
2. The brushing and pushing action of the legs pull the pelvis slightly forward as the torso inclines backward.

3. The focus turns to the left, away from the beat, as the leg brushes off the ground.
4. The arms are synchronized so that they help take the body up into the air.
5. The forward swing must be forceful and the back well arched.
6. The landing onto the bent leg is smooth and controlled, maintaining the connection in the buttocks and the extension of the spine.

Variation: Carbiole fouetté (fweh-TAY) is a whipped cabriole. Execute in the same manner as the cabriole, but after the bottom leg beats the top, quickly turn the focus fully over the left shoulder and then turn the body to face the direction you came from, landing in arabesque. Arms are overhead in 3rd position on the beat of the legs. They open to 1st position arabesque (L. arm forward, R. arm side) on the fouetté.

Changement

Changement (shahnzh-MAHN) is a change of feet while springing into the air. Begin in 5th position, right foot front. Plié on both legs. Spring upward into the air and change the legs so that the left foot is forward on the landing.

Mechanics:

1. Maintain connection in the buttocks as the knees bend and also on the landing. The torso should be perfectly straight with no rocking or arching in the body as it pushes upward or as it lands.
2. There must be a strong abdominal lift to go into the air.
3. The landing is controlled through the feet: tip of the toe, ball of the foot, and then heel.

Variations:

1. Turning inward. The changement is executed with a ½ turn. Begin in 5th position plié with the R. foot in front. Jump into the air and turn toward the front leg to the R., changing the legs while in the air. The R. leg will now be in back.
2. Turning outward. With the R. leg in front, spring into and turn away from the front leg and to the L. The left leg is now the forward leg. Note that there has been no actual change of the legs; rather the rotation of the body has caused the back leg to become the front leg.

Chassé

In the chassé (sha-SAY) step the back foot replaces the front. Begin by pointing the right foot forward and plié on the left. Transfer the weight forward onto the right foot. Begin to close the left leg to the right while springing into the air. Land on the left leg in plié as the right leg is extended to the front.

Mechanics:

1. On the spring upwards, the legs must come together into a tight sous-sus position while still in the air. The legs remain well turned-out from the hips and are stretched fully with the toes pointed. There is no space between the legs while in the air.
2. The landing of the back leg must be into a smooth controlled plié.
3. The chassé is not completed until the weight is transferred forward onto the R. leg. The movement does not stop over the back leg while landing from the sous-sus and is not a rocking step with the body weight falling forward and back. The movement is smooth and continuously traveling forward.

Variations: Chassés may be performed continuously in a series on one side or alternating R.L.R. to L.R.L. Chassés may also be performed traveling forward or back.

Emboîté

(ahn-bwah-TAY). Begin in 5th position with the right foot back. Spring into the air, bringing the right foot forward with the knee bent at 45°, while landing on the left leg in plié. Immediately spring into the air and land in plié on the right foot, with the left forward and bent 45° at the knee. The torso is erect and inclined slightly away from the body. The movement travels forward, alternating legs.

Mechanics:

1. The pelvis is held firmly in place by maintaining the connection in the buttocks and the lift in the abdominals, so that the hips do not sway from side-to-side on each landing.
2. The lifting leg remains well turned-out with the foot fully stretched.
3. The pushing leg must be fully extended under the torso before it lifts to the 45° angle in front.

Variations:

1. The legs can be lifted to the back. The torso will lean slightly forward, with the back arched. Be sure that the thighs are lifted in the turned-out position as the legs move to the low attitude.
2. The legs may be lifted to a 90° angle.
3. One can execute a series of half-turns, springing from one foot to the other, with the legs changing positions in the air. Turning to the R., spring into the air, landing in plié on the R. leg as you lift the L. leg in front and make a ½ rotation to the right. Spring off the R. leg onto the L. landing in plié, and bring the R. leg to the forward position while completing the second half of the rotation.
4. This movement may also be performed by bringing the foot to coupé position at the ankle instead of to 45° angle.

Entrechat Quatre

(ahn-truh-SHAH KA-truh). These are small beats of the legs. Begin in 5th position, right foot front and plié. Spring into the air and open the legs slightly to the side. Beat both calves so that the right leg crosses in back of the left. Open the legs slightly sideways again. Immediately bring the right leg in front as both feet descend to the floor, finishing in 5th position plié.

Mechanics:

1. When in plié before the push off and on the landing, be careful to keep both heels firmly on the floor.
2. Both feet push into the air at the same time, lifting the hip bones and fully stretching the legs to the tips of the toes.
3. This is a beat in which the legs open to the side and cross. The legs do not move forward and back to make the beat. It is essential that the connection in the buttocks is maintained and that there is maximum turn-out. If the buttocks release, distorting the position of the pelvis, it will be impossible to execute the beat to the side and across. Remember that the

legs must cross at the top of the thighs to properly perform the beating action.

4. The beat is done quickly so that the last crossing is finished as the legs begin to return to the floor.

Grand Fouetté

(fweh-TAY). When this movement is performed on the beam it is extremely difficult, requiring considerable control and a strong lift in the torso.

Begin standing on the left leg in plié, posed with the right leg extended to the front at a 90° angle. Deepen the plié and immediately straighten the leg and lift in relevé while lengthening the torso. Take the arms over the head while turning the right leg in the socket, making a ½ turn to the left, and finishing with the right leg in arabesque.

Mechanics:

1. The lifted leg will remain supported throughout the rotation. It remains at the established height before the fouetté. The lifted leg may be higher in arabesque but it will definitely not be lower.
2. The torso must lift considerably before turning and incline forward slightly, without dropping after the rotation, so that the leg has room to turn in the hip socket.
3. The head and focus will turn to the L., leading the rotation.
4. The lifted leg must remain fully stretched, both while it is to the front and after it rotates and becomes the back leg.

Fouetté Turning

This is the same movement as a grand fouetté but begins with a step and swing into the forward position. The leg then rotates in the socket without any pause. Step down into a plié on the left foot. Swing the right leg forward, lifting the arms over the head. Straighten the supporting leg and relevé, turning the head and hips to the left, and rotating the right leg in the socket so that it is in arabesque.

Variations

1. This may be completely reversed. Brush the R. leg directly behind into arabesque. Immediately turn the body to the R. and pull the R. hip back so that the leg turns in the socket and you have made a ½ turn, with the R. leg now in front.
2. Both fouettés may be executed as follows: begin and end in plié; begin in relevé and end in plié; begin in plié, spring into the air and land in plié; or step onto a relevé, stay in relevé during the rotation, and finish in plié.

Glissade

Glissade (glee-SAD) means to glide and refers to a traveling step. Begin in 5th position, with the right foot back and in plié. Glide the right foot along the floor to the side until it is fully stretched and pointed. Push away from the floor with the left leg so that both legs are momentarily stretched, with toes pointed. Transfer your weight as you land on the right leg in plié. Continue stretching the left leg until the pointed toe touches the floor to the side. Slide the left leg along the floor until it closes in 5th position front. The accent of the movement is on plié.

Mechanics:

1. Push off of the second leg at the moment the first foot leaves the floor. This happens only after the toe has been fully pointed to the side position.
2. Both legs should be extended to a 2nd position in the air before landing. Note that this is not a rocking step, transferring the weight from one foot to the other.
3. As the second leg closes, the first leg remains in plié. The second leg joins the first and only then do the legs straighten. If this is to be a preliminary movement for a second step of elevation, then the plié at the end of the glissade will be the beginning plié for the next movement.

Variations:

1. No change of feet. Begin with R. foot back and finish with R. foot back.

2. Change of feet. Begin with R. foot back and finish with R. foot front.
3. Glide to the side, back, or front.

Jeté

Jeté (zhuh-TAY) means "thrown" and is a jump from one leg to the other. The working leg has the appearance of being thrown as it brushes into the air. Begin in plié with the right foot in back. Slide the right foot along the floor to 2nd position. Just as the right foot is to leave the floor, simultaneously spring upward by pushing off with the left foot. Both legs are stretched in the air, thigh to toes. Bring the right leg underneath the torso and descend onto the right foot, landing in plié, replacing the left. The left leg finishes in back and bent, placed at the ankle of the right leg (coupé).

Mechanics:

1. Hold the torso erect and extended slightly forward. There is no transfer of weight. The torso remains in line with the placement of the pushing leg, the brushing leg moving under the torso to land.
2. The brushing of the working leg from 5th to 2nd position and the push from the second leg must be one continuous action with no pause until the landing.
3. Keep the connection in the buttocks to control the landing with a counter-pull upwards of the torso.
4. Both legs remain well turned-out during the movement.

Variation: This movement may be executed in place or traveling forward, to the side, or back.

Pas De Basque

(pah-duh-bask). This step is characteristic of the national or folk dances. The step alternately swings and moves from side-to-side in three counts.

Stand on the left leg. Swiftly raise the right leg to the left front position and bring the arms to 1st position. The right leg may be straight or slightly bent; the supporting leg is in plié. Swing the right leg, opening it to 2nd position. The moving leg will curve upward as it opens to about 90°. As the leg arrives in 2nd position, quickly jump into the air from the left foot, moving the arms up to 3rd position. Jumping onto the right foot, leg in plié, simultaneously developpé the left leg forward in the air. (The left toe passes the knee of the right leg before extending forward.) Let arms open from 3rd position over head to 2nd position. Lower the left leg to the floor, stepping onto the ball of the left foot, and quickly close the right foot to 5th position back in plié.

Mechanics:

1. There is considerable lift in the torso when both legs are off the ground from the first push off and before the first leg lands.
2. Be sure that the arms do not hike the shoulders up as they move to 3rd position.
3. Both legs remain well turned-out. Particular care is needed in opening the first leg to the 2nd position because the body is slightly crossed by the R. leg. As the leg opens, there is a tendency to leave the hip of the right leg lifted as it arrives in the second position. The hip of the lifted leg must rotate down and under so that the leg can move to the second position in proper alignment. Remember to pull the abdominals and hip bones up.

Variations: The pas de basque may be executed somewhat as a hitch kick by bringing the second leg up and across without going through the developpé position. Maintain the leg movement more or less to the front rather than opening the first leg out of the way to 2nd position.

Pas De Bourré

(pah-duh-boo-RAY). Begin by stepping onto the ball of the right foot, 5th position back. Immediately open the left foot to 2nd position, stepping onto the ball of the foot. Follow this by crossing the right foot over the left to step down on the right foot in plié. The left foot will come to coupé position back as the third step is taken.

Variation: The step may be done turning. Step onto the ball of the R. foot behind the L. Rotate the body half-way around to the R., while opening the leg to the L., and stepping into a small 2nd position. Pivot on the L. foot turning half-way around to the R. so that the R. foot closes in front of the L. Finish facing front.

Pas De Chat

(pah-duh-shah). This step is known as the "cat step" because of its quick and light spring into the air. Begin with the right foot back in 5th position. Plié on both legs. With a very sharp movement, pick the right foot up under the torso, bending the right knee, keeping the thigh turned-out, and pointing the toe. Immediately spring into the air with the knees pressed open and the toes together so that you are in the shape of a diamond. The right foot descends to the floor landing in plié. The left foot quickly follows the right so that it closes into 5th position in front of the right.

Mechanics:

1. The upper torso remains perfectly calm throughout the spring into the air. There is, however, some freedom of movement determined by the position of the arms. If the arms are held in 4th position front, then the torso would incline slightly forward and toward the curved front arm, with the head and focus directed out. That is, if the right leg is back, with the pas de chat traveling to the R., then the right arm would be curved in front of the body and the head turned to the R. If the arms are lifted up to 3rd position on the pas de chat, the torso would be held slightly forward from the hip line.
2. Execute counter-pull of the torso on the landing to keep a smooth transition.
3. The timing of the movement is uneven. It is almost as if the second leg was playing a game of tag with the first leg, both on the take-off and on the landing.

Pas De Cheval

(pah duh shuh-VAL). This movement is referred to as the "horse step" because of its similarity to a horse pawing the ground. The movement begins and ends with the foot pointed to 4th position front.

Beginning with the right foot pointed to the front, wipe the bottom of the foot on the floor as you pull the foot into the ankle of the left leg. Continue drawing the leg upward until the foot is pointed and slightly off the floor. Extend the foot back to the starting position by straightening the knee. Touch the toe to the floor. This action should be seen as one smooth continuous circle of the foot.

Mechanics: Both feet remain turned-out. The working foot must resist the floor as it draws into the ankle by pressing the ball of the foot and then the toes downward until the foot is fully stretched.

Variations:

1. The movement may begin on a straight leg but finish in plié as the working leg arrives in 4th position at the end of the movement. This is a nice movement on the beam. It also might be used to set the gymnast up for a pose leading into one or two changes of arms.
2. The movement may become a larger more grand movement by lifting the working leg all the way up to the knee of the supporting leg before executing a developpé forward and the point to the floor.
3. The supporting leg may spring into the air as the working leg draws into the ankle.

Royale

(rwah-YAL). This is very simply a changement with a beat before the change in the air. Begin in plié position with the right foot in front. As you spring into the air, open the legs slightly. At the height of the jump, close the legs tightly, beating the calves and insides of the thighs together with the right leg still in front. Then open the legs slightly so that the right leg can move to the back and land in plié.

Mechanics:

1. The pelvis must remain lifted with the hip bones raised so that the beat may be executed with proper alignment of the torso.
2. Shoulders remain calm and pulled down.
3. Legs are well stretched from thighs to toes.
4. There is a strong abdominal lift as the body springs up and a counter-pull in the torso as the body descends, so that the landing is smooth.

Sissonne

(see-SAHN). This is a strong movement of elevation and has many variations. It is excellent for both floor and beam and may be performed in all directions, with or without a change in feet. The finish may be with legs closed or open.

Sissonne Closed

For a sissonne closed, begin in plié position with the right leg front. Spring upward and forward into the air, pressing the right leg forward and extending the back leg to a low arabesque position as you jump. Land in plié position on the right leg; the left leg is still stretched into a low arabesque. Immediately close the left leg to the right by lowering the toe to the floor and sliding the foot along the floor to close in 5th position back, plié.

Mechanics:

1. There is a strong upward pull of the abdominals, but the torso will incline slightly forward and lift diagonally out as the body propels into space.
2. Both legs must be stretched from thighs to toes while in the air.
3. Counter-pull in the torso as the body lands so that the recovery is smooth.
4. As the R. leg bends on the landing, the hip bones must pull further upward, keeping the connection in the buttocks. Do not "sit" into the plié on the landing.

A sissonne open is executed in the same fashion as a sissonne closed, but the leg does not come to 5th position back on the landing. It remains in the low arabesque position so that the landing is on one foot.

Variations:

1. Sissonne closed and with a change of feet. Execute in the same manner but begin with the L. foot forward. Spring into the air immediately, switching legs so that the R. leg presses forward and the L. leg opens to low arabesque position.
2. Sissonne to the side. These may also be performed landing with the legs closed or open. The feet may change on the landing or remain the same. Begin in 5th position plié, R. foot front. Spring directly to the R. side, lifting the L. leg to the side position and raised about 45°. Land on the R. leg in plié and either leave the L. leg extended to the side position or close to 5th front or back.
3. Sissonnes traveling back, open or closed. The movement springs backward allowing the forward leg to lift about 45° to the front. This movement may also be performed with the switch of the legs. Begin R. foot front, 5th position. Plié and spring backward, extending the L. leg forward and pressing the R. leg back to land in plié.
4. Sissonne open with a change of legs. Begin with the L. foot in front and switch the legs so that the R. leg presses forward and the L. leg moves to arabesque. The landing is on the R. leg with the L. leg remaining in arabesque.
5. Sissonne fondu (fawn-DEW). Sissonne sinking down. It is performed like the sissonne closed, but instead of the leg closing in 5th position, it closes to coupé back.

6. Sissonne tombé (twan-BAY). Tombé means "to fall;" so this is sissonne falling. Perform this movement in the same fashion as sissonne open, but instead of leaving the leg in low arabesque, it will immediately swing forward as weight is transferred onto the leg in 4th position front (lunge). Begin R. leg front, 5th position, and plié. Spring into the air, pressing the R. leg forward and the L. leg to arabesque. Land on the R. leg in plié with the L. extended to arabesque. Swing the L. leg from back to front through 1st position and transfer the weight onto the L. leg in a lunge.

7. Sissonne turning. This will be a sissonne open and to the forward position but performed with a ½ turn at the spring into the air. Remember to lead the movement with the focus.

8. Sissonne relevé. Any of the sissonnes may also spring and land in relevé instead of plié. In relevé, the spring will not be as great but the lift must be even stronger, so that the sissonne appears to keep lifting upward on the landing. The torso must pull strongly out of the hips to maintain balance and the landing is preferably with an open leg. Lift into and onto the relevé so that the movement is sustained. Do not jump onto the relevé from above; this will take the movement down to the floor instead of extending up and out. The amount of spring onto the relevé must be carefully gauged so that the gymnast can continue pulling upward and out after landing on the ball of the foot.

For all forward sissonnes, holding the arms in an arabesque position, either 1st, 2nd or 3rd position, would be most natural. The arms might also be lifted to 1st on the spring and opened to 2nd on the landing. If 4th position is chosen and the sissonne is traveling forward and diagonally to the right, the right arm will extend to the side and the left arm will be rounded forward in 1st position. The focus and head will be turned to look back at where the movement has come from, and the torso will incline slightly forward and toward the rounded arm.

When the sissonne is to the back, a diagonal line is attractive. Lift the right leg to the front, and take the left arm forward in opposition, with the R. arm extended to the back. The torso may incline slightly forward with the movement.

Soubresaut

(soo-bruh-SOH). Soubresaut means to suddenly spring or bound forward. Begin in 5th position plié with the right foot in front. Strongly propel the body into the air by pushing the feet into the floor to take the torso both up and well forward. The legs must remain stretched, knees straight and toes pointed, with the right leg tightly in front of the left leg. The landing is made simultaneously on both feet in 5th position plié and with no change of legs.

Mechanics:

1. Because of the strong push up, and the distance traveled forward, particular care must be taken so the hips do not lose the connection and cause the body to "sit" on the landing.
2. There should be no rocking of the torso on take off. This is prevented by keeping the stomach and pelvis pulled up on the preparatory plié; also by controlling the rib cage on the take off. The rib cage must remain closed and the weight directed diagonally forward. Do not allow the back to arch by lifting the body from the upper part of the torso.
3. The legs do not separate during the jump but remain tightly crossed.

Variations:

1. The spring may be onto the balls of the feet in a tight sous-suś position.
2. The direction of the spring may be to the side, back, or forward.
3. Arms are optional.

Temps Du Poisson

(tahn duh paw-SAWN). This seems like another variation of soubresaut, but it is really a different step. It is called "the fish step" because of its similarity to a fish jumping out of the water. The back archs in the air so that the body forms a curve with the legs extended behind the feet, which are crossed to resemble a fish's tail.

Begin in 5th position plié, right foot forward. Strongly propel the torso into the air, throwing the legs backward and lifting the focus as the back is arched. Arms will go to 3rd position arabesque or to 3rd position over head. On the landing, the left leg will remain extended in the air and the right foot will come to the floor in plié position.

Mechanics:

1. The torso must propel forward and up just before the arching and the backward thrust of the legs. The movement travels forward in space, not just up and down.
2. This movement is more athletic in nature and must achieve a great deal of height and elevation to be well sustained.
3. By pulling the legs backward after the upward push off from the floor, the torso will experience a counterpull that lifts the body still further and causes the gymnast to appear momentarily suspended in air. There should be significant arch in the back while in the air.

Temps Levé

(tahn luh-VAY). This is simply a hop off of the supporting foot and back onto it again while the working leg is raised in any position. For example, spring forward into a sissonne, landing with the legs in an open position. Immediately spring upward from the forward leg and continue with another movement after the landing. Temps levé is a light springing movement that is excellent as a connecting step to vary the tempo or accent of another movement and is particulary useful on the beam.

Tour Jeté

(toor zshuh-TAY). This movement is generally performed with an introductory step or chassé to add impetus to the jump and turn in the air. It is also generally executed with the step or chassé beginning to the back, so that the body executes a half turn on the preparation into the jump. Standing on the right leg with the left leg pointed behind, turn to the left and step down onto the left leg into plié. Arms have opened from optional position to 2nd position. Brush the right leg forward as high as possible and simultaneously push off of the left leg, lifting the arms over head to 3rd position. At the height of the movement, turn the head to the left, over the shoulder, to spot the direction from which you have come. Turn the body to the left one half turn in the air, bringing the right leg underneath the torso to land in plié, while the left leg passes closely to the right in a scissors action so that it is held in arabesque on the landing. The arms open to 2nd position on the landing. In mid air the body should appear to be flung or turned over. This happens at the very height of the movement and should cause the body to appear to be momentarily suspended in air.

Mechanics:

1. The pushing of the supporting leg, the brush of the working leg, and the lift of the arms to 3rd position must all be coordinated so that they take the body up smoothly into the air.
2. The focus will lead the rotation of the torso by turning over the shoulder to look in the starting direction.
3. At the moment of rotation, the pushing leg should have lifted upward and joined the brushing leg, both being extended behind the body.
4. As the body rotates, the first leg pulls downward toward the floor to land in plié.
5. The legs remain close to each other at all times, the action of the legs being a scissors action; that is, they will move only up and down and not side to side. Instruct the gymnast to pretend this movement is executed within the confines of a long narrow hallway.

6. On the landing, the abdominal muscles and hip bones must remain well pulled up and the connection in the buttocks must be maintained so that there is no dropping of the torso.
7. The leg that is lifted to arabesque should not bob up and down on the landing but remain well stretched, toes fully pointed, with muscular contraction of the back and waist muscles to support the leg.
8. Keep the shoulders pulled down so that the lift is in the arms and the torso.

7

Choreography and the Floor Exercise Routine

Choreographing a floor routine is a creative process. As with the composition of music, painting, or any type of design, there is no one way of going about it. Certainly a sense of line and movement are essential tools of the choreographer, but any attempt to present a guaranteed method for composing a routine would be foolish or, at the very least, presumptuous. Still, some guidelines can be examined and presented with some possible approaches laid down. The final process of putting it all together will have to become the task of the individual, through continued trial, error, and experimentation.

UNDERSTANDING THE MUSICAL ACCOMPANIMENT

The gymnast's task is to present movement in the floor exercise routine that is appropriate and complements the rhythmic structure of the music.

Appropriate movement can be defined in two ways. First, the movement must be appropriate for the gymnast. This means that the movement must be suitable for her skill level and the style of the movement must complement her body type and personality. If the gymnast is technically incapable of performing a movement, it should be changed to something more suitable. An easier movement performed with confidence and skill is far more desirable than a more difficult movement performed tentatively.

Secondly, each gymnast has a quality of movement that is more naturally suited to a particular body type and ability. Common sense will determine the style of music that is best for each individual. If the gymnast is more lyrical in movement, has a sense of carriage and elegance in the arms, has high extensions and a strong arabesque, then a routine capitalizing on these balletic skills probably will be learned more readily and performed with more confidence than if the routine employed the more isolated movements of jazz. While jazz may present the perfect alternative for those gymnasts who feel awkward performing ballet, it is not the best choice for the gymnast who is beginning to develop physically and is uncomfortable with her new shape. She may feel inhibited by the strong hip and shoulder movements. Jazz is an explosive, exhilarating, out-going style of movement. It is better left to the gymnast whose personality and confidence are a match. Otherwise, the observer will be as uncomfortable with the performance as the gymnast.

Musical accompaniment that is strong and dramatic may be an excellent choice for the more mature gymnast, but the younger gymnast may lack the finesse necessary to perform this type of piece successfully. On the other hand, cute, bouncy, perky music, while "simply adorable" on that tiny, spunky little gymnast, is quite ridiculous on an older girl.

Very few gymnasts start each competitive season with a new optional floor routine. Rather they stay with one routine for two or even three years, making alterations in the skills as they improve, and perfecting the routine as it becomes more and more a part of them. Thus it is wise to pick music that the gymnast can grow with. When choosing new floor music, if it is evident that the gymnast is on the verge of blossoming into a young lady, then "Mickey Mouse on Parade" is probably better left to that cute little performer who can get some mileage out of the music.

There is one final thought to consider when choosing music, and that is the sanity of the judge. Whenever possible, stay away from popular music that is in vogue. Not only is the judge tired of seeing umpteen versions of the most popular fare of the season, but he or she is also likely to have developed a preconceived idea of what a routine to that particular music should be. At the very least, the gymnast is placed at a disadvantage because the judge, despite gallant efforts to remain impartial, may be inclined to compare one routine to another.

Movement must fit the rhythmic structure of the music, which is determined by the measurement of time known as a "beat." This is the underlying pulse which remains constant throughout the music. This beat is sometimes very obvious, as in a marching band that moves to the pulse of the drums, for example. At other times, the underlying beat may not be so obvious and one must "sense" the beat. The rate of speed or interval of each underlying beat establishes the tempo of the music. This may be fast or slow but generally remains constant.

Musical notes are grouped together by measures. That is, there are so many beats to a measure. The time measurement for music can be any of several combinations. The beat of the music might be measured or counted in 2, 3, 4, or 6. This is not so overwhelming as one might think. It is quite natural for us to group any repetitive sound into some type of unit. The dripping of a leaky faucet is a good example. The frequency of each drop corresponds to the beat in a musical phrase. Listening to the dripping of the faucet, a beat is established. These beats can be grouped into a unit which has numerical value. So the beating may become counts of:

1 2   1 2   1 2, or

1 2 3   1 2 3   1 2 3, or

1 2 3 4   1 2 3 4   1 2 3 4

These beats represent a measurement of time in music and they remain constant throughout the piece. In the first example, there are 2 counts or 2 beats to the measure. The second example has 3 counts or 3 beats. This measurement of time is common to a waltz but does not automatically imply that the music is waltz music. In the last example, there are 4 counts or 4 beats to the measure.

To continue with the leaky faucet example, the mind seems to hear one of the drips as being louder than the others. In other words, one of the beats seems to be accented. The drops of water are all falling at the same rate of speed and at even intervals. This rate of speed represents the tempo. Giving an accent to one of the drops of water or beats does not change the time or the tempo of the musical phrase but simply keeps the sound from becoming monotonous.

This is exactly what is done with movement. It must fit into the musical phrase or tempo of the music but it may accent the music by moving *with* the beat, *between* it, or *through* it.

Although movement must fit and complement the music, it is not limited to any rhythmic pattern found in that music; movement is limited only by the underlying beat or tempo.

Let us look at a steady 4 count measure of moderate tempo with a strong accent on the 1st beat of the measure.

1 2 3 4   1 2 3 4

With a simple walking step, this pattern can be complemented by stepping evenly on each beat in the music.

walk R.L.R.L.   R.L.R.L.

But this does not correspond to the rhythmical accent in the example phrase. To complement the accent in the music the first step might be made larger than the others by using a small leap instead of a step. There is now a walking pattern that has 4 counts or beats to the measure, with the first beat getting the accent. Although this is not as monotonous as 4 walking steps with no accent, it certainly is not going to raise anyone to his feet. But don't despair. Once the beat and accent are established, anything can be done to spice it up. The variations are endless.

In the first example, the movement was on each beat. Now see how the movement can be *between* the beats by changing the last walking step to chassé.

<u>1</u>   <u>2</u>   <u>3</u>   <u>and</u>   <u>4</u>

R. L. R. L.   R.
Leap   chassé

In this example there are 4 beats to the measure with an extra movement between the 3rd and 4th beat. Notice that this did not change the tempo of the measure (the time interval between the 3rd and 4th beats), nor did it affect the rhythmical accent that was already established.

In this example there are 3 steps of equal time with the first beat accented by taking a larger step. Note that in this first step, the legs will have to move more quickly in space than in the following two steps because more distance must be covered in the same amount of time. By adding the chassé, an additional accent is added to the music without changing the tempo.

The chassé moves between the counts and the space between the 3rd and 4th beat is referred to as an "and." This tells us that 3 steps or movements take place within 2 even counts.

We can also move through the counts by staying in one position longer than one beat, or by performing a movement that requires more than one beat to accomplish. For example, take another walking step on the left foot, turning or spinning on the right for two counts, and dropping to one knee to finish the 4th count. The whole phrase is performed in this manner:

<u>1</u>   <u>2</u>   <u>3</u>   <u>and</u>   <u>4</u>   <u>5</u>   <u>6</u>   <u>7</u>   <u>8</u>

R. L. R. L.   R.   L. R.   L.
Leap   chassé   stp. turn kneel

In this 8 count phrase, the music supplied a measure of 4 even beats with the first beat of the measure accented. Without changing the tempo of the music, the move is *with* the count; both the music and the movement accent the first beat of the measure. Moving *between* the beats is accomplished by the chassé (3 *and* 4). In the second measure, the music is still accented on the first beat but we choose to underplay this by simply taking a preparatory step and then turning *through* the next 2 beats of the music and finally giving additional accent to the last beat by showing contrast in levels and finishing on one knee.

Movement is simply another form of communication. It is accented and punctuated in much the same manner as a sentence. Just as several statements are combined to make up a paragraph, so it is with the steps. They combine to make up a movement phrase which communicates a thought, action, feeling, or emotion. In the same way that one emphasizes or accents a word in a sentence, parts of the movement are accented. Changing the emphasis without changing the steps will enhance, detract, or otherwise alter the quality of the movement.

The leap, chassé, turn, connecting walks, and the kneel, or other steps, can be combined and accented in any manner chosen. The less predictable the movement is, the more interesting it will be. While it is necessary to move to the music, complementing it and staying within its rhythmical structure, it is not necessary to move *with* the beat or be limited to the accents inherent in the musical phrase given.

CREATING THE DESIGN

Movement exists in space. For the gymnast, that space is predetermined in the form of the floor exercise mat. This is the performing area, and the floor routine must enhance and complement this dimension through design.

Tumbling passes are performed on the diagonal, but the rest of the routine is not limited to this dimension. The potential for use of the area is quite challenging, and how the floor routine develops in the form of spatial design will dramatically affect the overall composition.

Movement can be repeated, changed, or altered by virtue of a directional change of the body or the path of travel.

Movement Paths

Straight lines: Two dimensional. Movement progresses forward or backward along a straight line.

Diagonals: Diagonal movement is stronger than a straight line because it appears to "cut" through space.

Zigzag: This combines diagonals and gives a movement a jabbing quality; the performer appears to dart from angle to angle.

Square: Movement phrases repeated at right angles. This encloses the space with a controlled precision.

Of course the previously described straight line combinations, do not exhaust the potential for geometric designs within the routine.

A number of circular patterns can be used:

Circle: Obviously the most complete of curved lines. Smooth and fluid.

Figure eight: Variations of the circle, adding a little more interest and contrast in design.

Spiral: More dramatic in its accumulative effect, whether gathering speed and momentum, becoming larger or smaller, widening the scope, or creating more intensity.

Designs in space can be created by the path of travel and with the body, by the step or movement chosen. This can be further developed by reinforcing the pattern of design through the use and positioning of the arms, shoulders, legs, etc.

CHOOSING THE MOVEMENT

The style of dance performed will be determined, first, by the musical accompaniment. A Czardas, for example, will require movement that describes the flavor of folk dancing. Once the decision of style has been made, the movement should remain consistent with that choice throughout the entire routine. Regardless of whether the gymnast is performing dance steps or transitionary movements on the floor, if folk dancing and folk music has been chosen, then that flavor must prevail throughout the routine. The arms, head, and hand positions should consistently reflect the folk style in poses and floor positions, as well as dance steps; any turns and leaps chosen to fulfill the floor requirements must also be performed in a manner consistent with the folk style.

In establishing style, it is helpful to utilize a recurring theme in the movement, particularly if that theme is suggested in the music. Sharp, staccato, dramatic music might suggest movement that is angular. This angular movement could then be reflected both in the steps chosen for the routine and in the form and carriage of the body; the accompanying arm positions would be angular and perhaps harsher in their movement. The path of travel in the floor pattern might further develop this theme through angular and sharper floor designs with sudden changes of direction and levels. By contrast, lyrical music requires more fluid movement in the floor exercise routine.

A theme in the music can also be carried throughout the routine in the form of movement variations. This is accomplished by choosing a dominant movement to serve as the movement phrase. With lyrical music, for example, a swinging pattern might prove to be an appropriate part of the movement phrase. The gymnast might begin her routine, momentarily posed, moving only the arms in a circular pattern. Later, this same design of the arms could be used in combination with complementary dance steps; acrobatic skills can further carry the design by virtue of their path of travel. The floor work in the routine can also be complemented by using the same arm pattern that was established earlier in the routine.

METHODS FOR DEVELOPING THE THEME

Any number of methods may be used to develop the repetitive movement of a theme. You might choose a particular combination of steps in the form of a four count phrase that recurs throughout the routine. Or you might choose a distinct style of movement or distinct manner of carrying the head that can serve as the method for incorporating the repetitive movement. The theme should not, however, be repeated continually in exactly the same form; rather, an element of the chosen theme, such as a particular step, may serve as the basis for developing the dominant theme or variation throughout the routine.

The music itself can prove to be an excellent source for ideas and usually will contain some kind of repetitive pattern. Sometimes it is a recurring musical phrase or rhythmic pattern, sometimes the repetitive pattern is simply the style of the music itself, e.g., percussive or lyrical.

The theme that is chosen might be the *manner* of the movement rather than the actual movement itself, such as contrast. Perhaps the music repeatedly fluctuates between a lyrical phrase and a staccato one, or perhaps the contrast is between dynamic and bold musical accompaniment and soft, lyrical, mellow music patterns. This contrast may be reflected either through the movement itself or through the design of the floor pattern.

Regardless of which methods are used to develop the recurring theme in the composition, keep in mind these points:

- Any movement, pose, or combination of steps should be viewed from all directions and angles. It cannot be known from which position the audience or judges will view a routine; therefore, it should be visually attractive from all sides.
- The entire floor exercise mat should be used as creatively and comprehensively as possible. Try not to use the same area of the mat in the same manner more than once.
- Remember that sometimes *less* is *more*. Do not clutter movement with frivolous arm or leg positions and steps.

All positions and steps are important but not every position or step is the main theme in a phrase. Just as sentences have nouns, verbs, adjectives, main ideas, and connecting words, so has movement. Therefore, while *all* movement is important, not *all* of the movement will always be emphasized. Remember also that movement exists in levels of space from the elevated leaps to the horizontal movement on the floor. This adds interest and contrast to the composition.

Movement has:	form
	style
	spatial design
Movement can be:	percussive
	sustained
	lyrical
Tempo can be:	syncopated
	rhythmically irregular
	fast
	slow
	moderate
Movement can be:	dynamic
	explosive
	accented
	intense
	expressive
Style can be:	ethnic (folk)
	balletic
	abstract
	contemporary
Floor patterns can be:	diagonal
	sequential
	circular

8

Jazz Dance

Unlike ballet, jazz has few structured steps or movements and no standardized vocabulary. Jazz dancing is less restricted in its technique than ballet and its movements are explosive. With the introduction of varied musical accompaniment to competitive floor exercise, the use of jazz dancing as an interpretation of the music and a style of movement will become more and more pronounced. The piano as sole musical accompaniment has proved quite suitable for floor routines performed to "blues" music, generally interpreted with the controlled movements of the more "lyrical" jazz style. But the piano as sole accompaniment is less appropriate for the fast paced staccato or explosive style of jazz, which is more suitably performed to the rhythmic accompaniment of percussive drums. The following chapter offers some guidelines for understanding and experimenting with this style of jazz work.

Jazz dancing is an American dance form born of African heritage. The characteristic quality of jazz is that it is ever changing and is truly a physical interpretation of the musical sound of "jazz." There can be no jazz dance without jazz music. As the sound of jazz music has changed and developed, so has the dance. From the early music of Scott Joplin and a kind of ragtime dance, through the jitterbug to the present, jazz music and dance are constantly changing and refining.

Jazz dance has as many styles as it has performing outlets. It is found in musical theatre, television, and Las Vegas night clubs, where noted choreographers and teachers have developed their own unique styles and techniques. More recently, jazz dancing has gained a credibility previously lacking as it finds its place in the arts through the choreography and performance of major ballet companies.

It is this wide range of interpretation and lack of definite style that makes

jazz dancing most difficult to teach and understand. The "technique" of jazz generally evolves from the warm-up exercises performed at the beginning of a jazz class. Besides the obvious purposes of developing strength and flexibility, the exercises serve to increase body awareness and address the concept of isolating various body parts. The exercises also provide a certain tone or quality of movement through the use of the arms and torso. This is where "jazz style" is developed.

If the gymnast is interested in a serious study of jazz dancing, it is recommended that she enlist the aid of a qualified jazz teacher. There is no attempt here to go into a thorough discussion and interpretation of the various techniques and styles of jazz dance. Nor is there any attempt to simplify what jazz dance is; only to supply the gymnast with some basic tools for understanding and working with jazz dancing as a style of movement for floor exercise routines.

Although the fundamentals of ballet, such as spotting, placement, and correct muscular use of the body, are as applicable to jazz as they are to other forms of dance, the rhythm of jazz and the musicality of jazz movement cannot be put into words or explained in a book. As stated earlier, it is this lack of definite steps and patterns that make it necessary for jazz to be experienced visually. The intent here is only to give the reader some basic exercises and movements which will expose the gymnast to the principles of jazz dance. It is hoped that these principles will serve as a tool for developing steps and movements that reflect a jazz style and will prove helpful in the floor exercises or beam routines.

DISCOVERING THE RANGE OF MOTION

How one chooses to move the body will express a certain style or conjure up an image to the audience. The gymnast, through body language, can convey various attitudes and emotions. For example, movement can be coquettish, angular, dramatic, fluid, flirtatious; the descriptions are endless and all of these expressions can be related through the manner in which the individual moves. A certain tilt of the head may be coquettish. A walk may be direct and forceful, conveying a sense of urgency, or light and springy, expressing a feeling of light-heartedness. With this in mind, it is not the dance steps themselves that depict a certain style, but rather the entire impression that is related to the audience through consistently being aware of the total body picture.

Perhaps more than any other dance form, jazz dancing requires the controlled use of, and the fullest range of motion from, all the various body parts: the head, rib cage, pelvis, the joints of the wrists, the shoulders, and the hips. Warm-up exercises which incorporate the movements of these independent areas give jazz its distinct style. The exercises also lend flexibility to the joints and ligaments of the pelvis, hips, and shoulder regions; increase abdominal strength; and improve alignment of the torso and thoracic area.

THE BODY: POSITIONS OF JAZZ DANCING AND TYPES OF MOVEMENT

Head

full rotation—circle right or left
half head swing—semi-circle movement left to right or right to left
side tilt—ear to shoulder
vertical—forward up and down
horizontal—side-to-side chin over shoulder
neutral—focus directed outward, neck stretched, head erect

Hands and Wrist

wrist circles—right or left
fist—clenched hand
jazz hand—spread and extended fingers, straight wrist
heel press—flexed wrist, fingers extended
fan—fingers clenched and extended individually, starting with the thumb, and
  ending with the little finger

Pelvis and Hips

side—right or left
contract forward
release back
full circle—right or left
neutral—hips level

Torso and Spine

release—arch
contract—center back pulled, concave abdominal
twisting—from the waist right or left
bending—side stretch right or left
flat back (table top)—forward from the hips
neutral—head erect, focus out, and spine lengthened

Shoulders

up and down
forward and back
full rotation forward
full rotation back
neutral
(shoulder movement may be independent [one shoulder at a time]; alternate
  [shoulders move in opposition]; simultaneous [both shoulders together])

Quality of Movement May Be:

percussive—sharp, strong, rhythmic
lyrical—flowing, connected movements

SOME BASIC JAZZ POSITIONS AND MOVEMENTS

Figures 8.1 through 8.3 illustrate some basic jazz positions and movements.

Figure 8.1   *Jazz First position arms (feet in parallel first).*

Figure 8.2   *Jazz Second position arms (feet in parallel second).*

Figure 8.3   *Feet in parallel Fourth position.*

The jazz hand is a position of the hand in which the palm is facing forward and the fingers are extended with a straight wrist. See Figure 8.4.

Figure 8.4   *Jazz hand.*

Figures 8.5 through 8.8 illustrate additional jazz positions.

Figure 8.5   *Fourth position (lunge).*

Figure 8.6   *Side parallel lunge with torso twist.*

Figure 8.7   *Parallel passé position (at the knee).*

Figure 8.8   *Parallel coupé position (at the ankle).*

The jazz split is a slide to the floor which finishes with the forward leg straight and the back leg flexed. If the split is performed with the left leg in front, the left arm will reach to the floor and the right arm will extend diagonally upward. The body weight is held primarily over the back leg, which is flexed and turned outward. As the left hand reaches for the floor it catches the weight of the body and gently lowers the left hip to the floor. See Figures 8.9 and 8.10.

Figure 8.9   *Jazz split (half way down).*

Figure 8.10 *Jazz split (full).*

A hip lift is shown in Figure 8.11.

Figure 8.11 *Hip lift.*

A lay-out is a straight position from the pelvis to the head. Types of layouts are shown in Figures 8.12 through 8.14.

Figure 8.12 *Side lay-out*

Figure 8.13 *Forward lay-out.*

Figure 8.14 *Back lay-out.*

A knee spin is a turn done on both knees using the right and then the left leg separately to complete one rotation. The torso must remain erect, with the pelvis under the ribs. Standing on the left foot, place the right knee to the floor behind the left foot. Turn the body to the right as you bring the left knee to the floor to meet the right knee. Continue turning to the right, lift and open the right knee to the side as you step onto the right foot. Stand immediately. The action of the spin is quick and smooth.

A knee hinge is a very straight position of the torso in which the legs are parallel, the knees flexed, and the heels raised off the floor. There must be a strong abdominal lift and tucking of the pelvis so that there is a straight line from the knee to the top of the head. The bend of the knees may be slight, deep, or with the knees touching the floor. See Figure 8.15.

A hitch kick is a kicking of both legs in the same direction. First kick the right leg to the front. Before it can return, begin to kick the left leg up so that the kicking is a scissors action. Hitch kicks may be performed to the front, side, or back. Generally the second kick is the highest and is accented. The kicking legs may be straight, flexed, or flexed and extended to a straight position as in developpé.

Pas de bourre refers to three steps which may be taken in any direction. The knees are straight or bent, the feet flat or in relevé.

A seat spin is a turn while sitting on the buttocks with the knees flexed and together, the toes pointed. The hands are used to push the body around. Other variations of the legs may be used.

Figure 8.15   *Knee hinge.*

Possible Qualities of Jazz Movements

- lyrical—The movement is flowing. It connects smoothly from one phrase to the next.
- percussive—These are sharp, strong, and striking movements. They create accents to specific counts in the music.
- sustained—The movements are elongated. Transition is held briefly before going on to the next movement.
- thrust—Sharp accented movement of any part of the body generally with an isolation. The isolated part, striking out and being withdrawn quickly in a pulsing fashion.

ISOLATIONS

The ability to isolate body parts and move them independently is one of the basic characteristics of jazz dancing. The following isolations are presented as an exercise only. Their purpose is to teach the gymnast to move the various parts of the body independently or in opposition to another body part.

These exercises train the body's reflexes, coordination, and body awareness, which considerably increases the scope of movement.

Head Isolation Exercise

Starting position: Stand with feet parallel, spine lengthened, abdominal muscles pulled up, and buttocks contracted. Hold head in neutral position. Arms are at the sides, palms forward, elbows bent and pulled back.

Exercise:

1. Count 1: Drop head down so that chin is to chest. Count "and": Return to neutral position. Repeat this 4 times to the count of 4 with a sharp pulsing movement. Note that the head should stop completely for that moment while in the neutral position and focus should be directed out.
2. Count 1: Side tilt (drop head to right shoulder so that the ear is to the right shoulder). Count "and": Return to neutral position. Repeat this 4 times to the count of 4. Note that the shoulders do not move up to the ears.

Figure 8.16 *Head forward.*

Figure 8.17 *Head side tilt.*

3. Count 1: Turn head to right (focus is out over right shoulder). Count 'and": Return to neutral position. Repeat this 4 times to the count of 4. Note that the chin remains level.
4. Count 1: Look directly up to ceiling, pulling the head back. Count "and": Return to neutral position. Repeat this 4 times to the count of 4.

Figure 8.18 *Head turned to the right.*

Figure 8.19 *Head back.*

Once the pattern of the head isolations is learned, the exercise should be performed rapidly without stops. The movement should be precise, with only the head moving, and the rest of the body maintaining proper alignment. The exercise is performed first to the right and then immediately repeat to the left.

Head isolation exercise performed to counts as follows:

4 pulses forward	count 1-2-3-4
4 pulses side tilt (right)	5-6-7-8
4 pulses side (right)	count 1-2-3-4
4 pulses back	5-6-7-8

Immediately repeat to the left:

4 pulses forward	count 1-2-3-4
4 pulses side tilt (left)	5-6-7-8
4 pulses side (left)	count 1-2-3-4
4 pulses back	5-6-7-8

Repeat forward, side tilt, side and back in 2 counts both right and left. Repeat forward, side tilt, side and back in 1 count right and left.

Half head swing left to right	count 1-2
Half head swing right to left	3-4
Full head circle to the right	5-6-7-8

Half head swing right to left	1-2
Half head swing left to right	3-4
Full head circle to the left	5-6-7-8

Shoulder Isolation Exercise

Starting position: Stand with feet parallel (2nd position), spine lengthened, abdominal muscles pulled up, and buttocks contracted. Head erect and focus out. Arms at sides, palms and elbows pressed slightly forward, fingers spread apart.

Exercise #1: Thrusts

1. Count 1: Lift right shoulder straight up and toward the right ear. Count "and": Return to neutral position. Repeat this 4 times to the count of 4. Accent is up and on the count. Keep the torso extended. Hold the head still and move only the right shoulder.

Figure 8.20 *Right shoulder lifted.*

2. Count 1: Press right shoulder blade down, forcing the right arm slightly away from the body. Count "and": Return to neutral position. Repeat 4 times to count of 4. Accent is down on the count. Repeat parts 1 and 2 with the left shoulder.

Figure 8.21 *Right shoulder down. Notice that the shoulder blade is not only pulled firmly down toward the waist but is also engaging muscular action that pulls it out from the spine. This is necessary if the proper work in the thoracic area is to be achieved and a general flopping up and down of the shoulder avoided.*

Shoulder isolations exercise #1 performed to counts as follows:

Pulse right shoulder up 4 times	count 1-2-3-4
Pulse right shoulder down 4 times	5-6-7-8
Pulse left shoulder up 4 times	count 1-2-3-4
Pulse left shoulder down 4 times	5-6-7-8
Pulse right shoulder up 2 times	count 1-2
Pulse left shoulder up 2 times	3-4
Repeat with right shoulder	count 5-6
Repeat with left shoulder	7-8
Repeat alternately lifting right and left shoulders to single count—8 times.	count 1-8
Circle both shoulders together forward, up, back, and down	count 1-2
Repeat	3-4
Repeat	5-6

Repeat   7-8
Reverse circle—up, forward, down,   count 1-8
   and back—4 times

Remember that nothing is moving but the shoulders. Continue to keep the spine stretched and control the rib cage so that it does not press open as the shoulders circle. Be particularly careful to keep the jazz hand. (Palm flat, fingers extended, and fingers fanned open.) The elbows will remain pressed forward throughout the exercise.

Exercise #2:   Circles

1. Count 1: Press right shoulder forward, lift up, press back and pull down. (Shoulder describes one full circle.) Repeat 4 circles to count of 4. Movement of the circle is smooth and only the right shoulder is moving.
2. Count 1: Press left shoulder forward, up, back, and down. Repeat 4 circles with the left shoulder to count of 4.
3. Count 1: Circle left shoulder forward and up. Count "and": Circle right shoulder forward and left shoulder back. Count 2: Circle left shoulder back and right shoulder forward and up. The shoulder movement is now syncopated with the accent on the count of 2. Allow the body and ribs to tilt slightly into the right side with the last shoulder circle on count of 2.
4. Count 1: Circle left shoulder forward and up. Count "and": Circle right shoulder forward and left shoulder back. Count 2: Circle right shoulder back and left shoulder forward and up.

The accent is now to the left side and on the count of 2.

Should isolations exercise #2 performed to counts as follows:

4 circles with right shoulder	count 1-2-3-4
4 circles with the left shoulder	5-6-7-8
Syncopated right, left, right	count 1 and 2
Syncopated left, right, left	3 and 4
Syncopated right, left, right	5 and 6
Syncopated left, right, left	7 and 8
Repeat	count 1-16

Reverse and repeat. Begin right shoulder up, forward, down, and back. Accent will be forward. Reverse syncopated shoulder movement in the same manner.

Throughout the exercise the hips remain still. Be particularly careful that the head does not bob about on the syncopated movement. The rib cage remains still on the individual circles and only gives in to the movement on the syncopation.

Rib Cage Isolation Exercise

Starting position: Stand parallel feet second position, knees slightly bent, spine lengthened, and abdominal muscles pulled up. Buttock muscles are contracted. Hands on hips (elbows forward, palms flat against pelvis).

Exercise

1. Count 1: Slide rib cage directly right. Count "and": Return to neutral position. Repeat 4 times to the right, keeping shoulders level. Hips remain still.

Figure 8.22 *Rib isolations. Ribs are pulled on a level plane to the side while the hips remain stationary.*

2. Count 1: Slide ribs directly to the right. Count "and": Slide ribs directly left. Count 2: Slide ribs directly right. Continue syncopated movement so that it alternates R.L.R., L.R.L., etc.
3. Count 1: Slide rib cage directly left. Count "and": Return to neutral position. Repeat 4 times to the left.
4. Count 1: Press rib cage directly forward. Count "and": Return to neutral position. Repeat 4 times. Note that only the ribs move, while the hips remain still. The shoulder blades will contract downward and press into the back as the ribs move forward.

5. Count 1: Contract ribs inward. Count "and": Press ribs forward. Count 2: Contract ribs inward. The movement of the ribs front and back is now syncopated. Repeat with 2 sets, alternating in this manner: back, front, back. . . . front, back, front. . . . etc.
6. Count 1: Contract rib cage inward. Count "and": Return to neutral position. Repeat 4 times. Movement to the back is slight.
7. Count 1: Contract rib cage inward. Count "and": Contract back. Count 2: Press forward. Continue alternating for 2 sets: front, back, front; then back, front, back. Throughout the entire exercise, the waistline remains stretched upward and abdominal muscles remain contracted.

Rib cage isolation exercise performed to counts as follows:

Pulse ribs to the right 4 times	count 1-2-3-4
Syncopate left, right, left	5 and 6
Syncopate right, left, right	7 and 8
Pulse ribs to the left 4 times	count 1-2-3-4
Syncopate right, left, right	5 and 6
Syncopate left, right, left	7 and 8
Contract ribs inward 4 times	count 1-2-3-4
Syncopate front, back, front	5 and 6
Syncopate back, front, back	7 and 8
Circle rib cage 4 times, starting right front side, back, side	8 counts
Circle 4 times to the left front, side, back, side	8 counts

Hip Isolation Exercise

Begin in the same position as described for rib cage isolations. This exercise is performed in exactly the same manner, but with the hips substituting for the ribs. The knees must be slightly bent throughout the exercise to allow for free movement of the pelvis. When the pelvis presses forward, there is an upward pull of the abdominal muscles and a contraction of the buttocks muscles. Backward movement of the pelvis is actually a release of the lower spine.

USING ISOLATIONS WITHIN A MOVEMENT PHRASE

As stated earlier, isolations are an integral aspect of jazz dancing. Working with these isolations and warm-up exercises increases the gymnast's general sense of how the body moves to achieve a jazz style. Breaking down a particular jazz movement and attempting to put into words exactly how these isolations come into play is quite tedious; moreover, describing each position independently is wordy and interferes with the spontaneity that is the very essence of jazz. If the gymnast is encouraged to practice these isolations, though, she will find that the movements will soon become automatic, giving her the ability to add them to dance steps when a jazzy feeling to the movement is preferred. To illustrate, try the following combination.

Starting position:

1. Feet: stand on R. foot (attitude a'terre). Cross L. leg behind R. and place ball of the foot on the floor. Front of L. thigh is pressed into back of R. leg. Both legs are slightly bent.
2. Arms: Long jazz arm position at sides of body, with palms flat (fingers extended) and pressed forward. Shoulder blades pulled down in back.
3. Head: Turned to R.; focus over R. shoulder.

Exercise:

1. Count 1: Thrust R. shoulder up. Count and: Thrust L. shoulder up and R. shoulder down. Count 2: R. shoulder up, L. down.

Figures 8.23 through 8.28 *Photos accompany study combination. Position shown is the first step of the ball change. (Weight is on the left foot. Be sure to finish the ball change with the weight on the right foot.)*

2. Count 3: Open L. leg to 2nd position and fall into side parallel lunge (L. knee bent, R. leg straight). Arms raised over head to make diamond shape (palms face out).

3. Count 4: Push off L. foot to balance on R. leg. L. leg is turned in passé position (L. toe to R. knee). R. knee is bent slightly. Arms: Move down to original position. Head: Focus changes from over R. shoulder to forward.

4. Count 5: Step down on L. foot behind R. and ball change (L.R.).

5. Count 6: Pivot ½ turn to L. raised onto the balls of both feet. Arms: reach straight upward. Focus: up.

6. Count 7: 1 full circle of the head to the **R**.
7. Count 8: Contract arms and body down over legs; bend knees.

In this study combination several body isolations are combined through syncopated counts, contrasting movement, changes in level, changes in direction, and changes in intensity—all within 8 counts. Despite these apparently abrupt changes, the movement must remain fluid and smoothly controlled so the transitions do not take on a mechanical or disjointed appearance.

Combination analysis:

Counts 1 and 2: The shoulder thrusts are sharp, clear movements, strongly accenting the up position on the first and second counts. *The strength of the shoulder isolations make a strong statement and the focus must not appear hesitant or it will contradict the movement.*

Count 3: Everything happens at once here, and it is purely a transitional movement. It should be softly underplayed but not thrown away. The movement is timed so that the change in focus, the diamond position of the arms, and the lunge *all* arrive in their position at the same time. The arms have the furthest distance to travel in space, so they will have to initiate the movement.

Count 4: Again everything changes at the same time but the accent is up. There must be a contrasting distinct level change from the opened downward lunge of the transitionary count of 3 to the strong and sustained upward lift of the accented count 4. Once again the arms have the furthest distance to travel in space, so they will initiate and slightly lead the movement.

Count 5: This should appear more as a little "breath" than anything else. It is light and serves to prepare and give impetus to the following movement, which is a level change and a directional change.

Count 6: We can liken this movement to the exclamation point in a sentence. There is a slight spiral into the relevé while pivoting left. The body is fully stretched and extended upward, spine lengthened. The focus and the arms are lifted. The torso must be tight to maintain balance. Note that the head will lead the movement by spotting to the end position of the relevé. So from the ball change of count "and 5," the focus will turn over the left shoulder and direct upward followed by the change in the direction of the body (pivot ½ to left). Always remember that leading directional changes with the focus will add clarity to the movement as well as balance and control.

Count 7: The head circle is quick and follows immediately on the heels of count 6, so that it is a smooth continuation of the relevé and adds suspension to the lift. To maintain balance during the head circle, direct focus outward at eye level, looking at a point in space in front of you.

Count 8: There is a sudden change of level and intensity from the strong upward reach to a complete drop and relaxation of the body.

The purpose of this study combination is to show how isolations can be put together to comprise a movement, and how changes in levels, intensity, and accents will lend interest to any movement phrase. One or more of these elements can be altered without changing the basic pattern of the movement. The counts may be adjusted to make a 12 count or a 16 count combination. This alone would change the rhythm of the combination, which would then alter the mood. What is important to understand is that any movement pattern will contain one or more of these elements and the gymnast must learn these along with the mechanics of the steps. Otherwise, the movement becomes dull and uninteresting to watch.

Tables 8.1 and 8.2 show examples of the type of coordination exercises frequently used in jazz warm-ups. The purpose of these exercises is to teach the student to move independent body parts in opposing directions.

Note that the movement in Part A of the coordination exercise is clear, precise, and well defined. Arm movements are strong and there is a feeling of energy coming from the fingertips. Do not break the line of the arm by bending over. After the coordination of the arm movements is successfully accomplished, add to the exercise the leg movement described in coordination exercise: Part B.

Table 8.1 *Coordination Exercise:* *Part A*

Beginning position: Arms extended out to sides (horizontal); palms forward; jazz hands

The Counts	The Movement: Right Arm Position	The Movement: Left Arm Position	Photo Figures
Count 1	Contract R. elbow, bringing palm in front of the chest (horizontal)	L. arm remains extended to the side horizontal pos.	See Figure 8.29.
Count 2	R. arm moves to vertical pos., elbow down, palm up (palm facing face)	At the same time, contract L. elbow so that palm is in front of chest. L. arm is horizontal.	See Figure 8.30.
Count 3	Turn R. palm outward as you slide hand directly up until it is reaching over head (sliding up an imaginary wall)	At same time, change L. arm to verticle pos. (arm still bent). The palm turns to face outward.	See Figure 8.31.
Count 4	Keeping the elbow straight, open the R. arm from the extended verticle pos. over head, directly side to horizontal pos.	At the same time, slide the L. hand up the imaginary wall to reach arm overhead (vertical).	See Figure 8.32.

Figures 8.29 through 8.32 *Photos accompany coordination exercise part A.*

Table 8.2 *Coordination Exercise: Part B*

Beginning position: Stand in 3rd or 5th position, **R.** foot back; arms extended to sides (horizontal pos.)

The Counts	The Movement of the Legs	The Movement of the Arms	Photo Figures
Count 1	Point tendu the **R.** foot directly to the side	Contract **R.** elbow, palm to chest, arm horizontal	See Figure 8.33.
Count 2	Flex **R.** foot at the ankle	Change **R.** arm to vertical, contract **L.** arm to chest, horizontal (both arms bent)	See Figure 8.34.
Count 3	Point tendu **R.** foot	Extend **R.** arm over head (palm out) change **L.** arm to vertical	See Figure 8.35.
Count 4	Close **R.** foot 3rd or 5th pos. front	Open **R.** arm directly side to horizontal. Extend **L.** arm reaching over head (vertical). Both arms are facing out.	See Figure 8.36.

Continue exercise, traveling forward, repeating the arm movements exactly as described while pointing and flexing the left foot. Continue in this fashion for a total of 4 sets or 32 counts. Then repeat the entire exercise traveling to the back by pointing the left foot first and closing the left leg to the back. As this is done, the arms will begin with the contraction of the left elbow first. Remember to keep all movements clear, sharp, and precise.

Figures 8.33 through 8.36 *Photos accompany coordination exercise part B.*

SOME JAZZ STEPS

Triple

A movement is considered to be a triple any time that three steps are taken to two counts of music. The movement alternates from the right foot to the left and would be counted "3 and 4" (syncopation). The direction to be traveled may be forward, back, side, or turning. The steps taken may be any combination of flat foot, relevé, bent, or straight leg. The steps may be slow walks or quick runs and the combinations are quite varied. The movements may be used as traveling steps, as connecting steps, or as preparatory steps for turns or leaps. Specific steps that fall under the category of a "triple" are pas de bourré, chassé, waltz, or step ball change. Of course the flavor of any of these steps can be altered by the choice of arm position, by adding contractions, or by incorporating into the movement isolations of the head, pelvis, shoulders, etc.

Following are some triples for the team to practice in the same manner that they would work on tumbling skills. Different acrobatic moves may be substituted to fit the skill level of the team.

Triplet combinations:

Traveling forward and alternately placing one foot in front of the other.

DOWN indicates that the step is taken onto a flat foot with the knee slightly bent. UP indicates that the step is taken onto a straight leg and on the ball of the foot.

Triplet exercise #1:

DOWN	UP	UP	DOWN	UP	UP
L.	R.	L.	R.	L.	R.
1	&	2	1	&	2

Triplet exercise #2:

DOWN	UP	DOWN	DOWN	UP	DOWN
L.	R.	L.	R.	L.	R.
1	&	2	1	&	2

Triple exercise #3:

DOWN	DOWN	UP	DOWN	DOWN	UP
L.	R.	L.	R.	L.	R.
1	&	2	1	&	2

Acrobatic-triplet combination:

traveling forward	DOWN	UP	UP	DOWN	UP	UP
	R.	L.	R.	L.	R.	L.
	1	&	2	2	&	2

turning (1 full turn)	DOWN	UP	DOWN
forward on R. Then ½ turn	R.	L.	R.
to L. stepping on L. behind	3	&	2
R. Then ½ step forward on R.			
Over L. to step forward on R.			

Hop R. step down on L., kick	SIDE	AERIAL
R., land R.	4	& 2

After landing from the aerial, prepare L., and begin the triplet starting R. (DOWN UP UP). The object of the exercise is to move smoothly in and out of the acrobatic tricks while giving equal consideration to both the dance step and the gymnastic skill.

Adding arms to the movement:

1. Count 1: R. arm lifts to 1st pos. (front) and 2: R. arm opens to 2nd pos. (side)
2. Count 2: L. arm lifts to 1st pos. (front) and 2: L. arm opens to 2nd pos. (side)
3. Count 3: Arms cross at wrists in front of chest and 2: keep wrists crossed as you raise arms over head and then open

Split leap-triplet combination:

traveling forward	DOWN	UP	DOWN
	R.	L.	R.
	1	&	2

	DOWN	SPLIT LEAP	LAND
	L.	R.	R.
	1	&	2

The exercise continues across the floor, alternating the leap each time. Arms are optional.

These are just two examples to show how the arm and leg movements of a specific dance step might be combined with a gymnastic skill or leap. Remember that a triplet is three steps to two beats and may be counted in whatever manner is comfortable: 1-2-3, 2-2-3, 1 and 2, or 1-2-3, 1-2-3. It is helpful to teach the arm movements and the leg movements separately, particularly if the coordination of the exercise is complex, so that the gymnast understands the line and carriage of the body as well as the timing of the movement.

What to watch for:

1. The quality of the movement should be smooth, the arms fluid. Remember that the arms add style to the triplet, balance to the turn, and should be so timed as to give impetus to the leaps.
2. Focus. The focus should always be directed toward the line of travel, with eyes raised. Looking down at the floor during the dance steps is a bad habit that is usually born out of a lack of self-confidence. Encourage the gymnast to always be aware of where the focus is. Allowing the eyes to wander aimlessly during the movement gives the appearance of uncertainty. Remember, the focus lifts up when the body goes up. If the body is directed upward into a leap, but the focus is directed down toward the floor, you have a conflict.
3. Carriage of the body. The chest is lifted and open and the torso is fully stretched. Watch that the torso does not collapse each time the knees bend on the triplet. Encourage the gymnast to be aware of her presentation.
4. Preparations. Prepare for the turn or leap with sufficient bend of the knees to propel the body upward.
5. Landing from the leap. Controlled landing with sufficient bend of the knees will act as a shock absorber for the spine. There should be no jarring or jerking of the body. This is also accomplished by lengthening the spine upon landing, rather than collapsing into the ground.
6. Feet. When stepping down on the triplet do not step heel first. Feet are fully pointed while in the air and the toes press the floor away on the leaps.
7. Shoulders. Shoulders do not lift when the arms lift, but remain firmly pulled down so that the line of the neck and chest is not destroyed. Lengthen the neck so that the ears are stretched away from the shoulders.
8. Arms and hands. Encourage the gymnast to feel the energy extending out through the finger tips. Watch that the arms are correctly placed during the exercise. The position of the arms may be arbitrarily chosen but insisting that they are placed in a specific position teaches one to be aware of where the arms are in space, which will improve the overall performance.

9. Leaps. Leaps should be fully stretched, knees straight, toes pointed, hip bones lifted in front, focus directed up and out.
10. General body placement. Keep the abdominals working, spine extended, and buttocks muscles connected.

Chassé

This is a traveling step when one foot chases the other out of its position. Chassés may be performed traveling forward, side, or back. The first step of the chassé is on the flat foot with the knee slightly bent. The next movement is in the air with the legs stretched so that the thighs are touching, one in front of the other, and the feet are pointed. The landing is then on the back leg with the knee bending slightly to cushion the landing. When the chassé is executed to the back, you simply reverse this process.

Example #1: Chassés performed in a series:
Traveling forward with the right foot remaining in front of the left.

R. L. R.	L. R.	L. R.	L. R.
1 & 2	& 3	& 4	& 5

Arms: Optional. Example: L. arm forward, R. arm side, or both arms side

Example #2: Chassé alternating:
Traveling diagonally forward to the right (R. front) and diagonally forward to the left (L. front).

R. L. R.	L. R. L.	R. L. R.	L. R. L.
1 & 2	1 & 2	1 & 2	1 & 2

Arms: Same as previous exercise, but alternating in opposition to legs.

What to watch for:

1. Sous-sus. In both of these examples the legs will come to the sous-sus position in the air, with both legs straight and touching, one in front of the other, and the feet fully extended.
2. Feet. Step toe first, not heel first or flat-footed.
3. Focus. Lifted slightly and directed toward the line of travel. Note that in #2 the focus is diagonally forward to the left.
4. Torso. Maintain correct body placement.
5. Recovery. The landing is kept smooth and controlled by bending the landing leg following the sous-sus in the air.
6. Transfer of weight. As the gymnast lands from the sous-sus the weight is

transferred smoothly onto the forward step. One must continue to press the body weight in the direction of the line of travel to prevent any rocking back and forth. Although the footwork is front foot, back foot, front foot, the body must continue to move forward in space through all three steps.

Example #3:   Side jazz chassé:
With feet in parallel position, travel sideways.

step side with R. foot	ball of L. foot beside R.	open R. foot side
1	&	2

Knees remain relaxed. Initiate movement from the hips by pressing the right hip over the right leg. Both knees and feet remain parallel. This chassé differs from the previous two in that the movement remains closer to the ground. As the 3rd step is taken, allow the left knee to turn inward so that the ankle and inside of the left foot are turned to the floor (somewhat of a dragging effect). Think of the left foot as being heavier.

Example #4:   Jazz chassés with pas de bourre turning:
Feet parallel and traveling sideways.

jazz chassé	pas de bourre turn cross behind with L., over with R., forward with L. (1 full turn)	jazz chassé	pas de bourre turn
R. L. R.	L. R. L.	R. L. R.	L. R. L.
1 & 2	3 & 4	5 & 6	7 & 8

Arms: Optional.

What to watch for:

1. Knees. Somewhat relaxed so that movement remains "into" the floor.
2. Hips. The hip presses over the right leg on the chassé.
3. Torso. Although the knees are somewhat bent, the spine remains extended and there is a feeling of tension or contained energy in the body.
4. Pas de bourre turn. The turn is sharp but does not begin to rotate until the 2nd step of the pas de bourre. The turn is actually begun on the "and" count.
5. Weight transfer. Body weight is always pressing toward the line of travel regardless of the direction of the step (side, back, or turning). This should give the pas de bourre turn the characteristics of a low running step.
6. Focus. Here the focus remains straight out on the chassé (not over the R. shoulder toward the line of travel). The focus will not change until the 2nd step of the pas de bourre turn. On the 2nd step it will quickly turn

over the left shoulder and continue around to spot the direction of travel. After the turn and on the chassé, the focus will change to the outward or neutral position again.

Once the gymnast is able to move smoothly across the floor, alternating from the chassé to the pas de bourre turn, the sequence may be altered by adding a leap or acrobatic skill.

For example:

side jazz chassé	pas de bourre turn	side split leap
R. L. R.	L. R. L.	brush R., land R.

side jazz chassé	pas de bourre turn	full tour in air
		feet together and plié
R. L. R.	L. R. L.	(tour may be single or double)

Example #5:   Side jazz chassé with torso twist:
Executed in same manner as previous side jazz chassé. At the same time as the third step of the chassé, the torso is allowed to twist from the waist to the direction of travel. If the chassé is to the right, the torso will twist ¼ to the right.

R. L. R.   twist upper body to R.
1 & 2
Arms: Right arm side, left arm forward.

The movement is still initiated with a pressing sideward of the hips. Body weight is primarily over the right foot and the left leg will be extended so that the position becomes a side lunge with the hips facing the direction of the knees and the upper torso. The shoulders are twisted ¼ past the hips. The chest remains open and lifted.
   This type of chassé is very useful as a preparation for a turn or directional change.

Example #6:   Jazz chassés with torso twist and inside pirouette:

R. L. R.	inside turn on R.	step down on L.
1 & 2	3	4

Arms:	L. arm forward	jazz first position	open arms side
	R. arm side		palms down

Focus is straight out on the chassé. As you step down on the right foot (3rd step of the chassé), change the focus over the right shoulder, spot for the pirouette, and finish with the focus out and the head in neutral position. Remember that the emphasis is down and that you are in plié on the right leg at the end of the chassé, which is your preparation for the turn. The turn is on the ball of the foot, but in a jazz turn there is the option of keeping the supporting leg slightly bent. It is an inside turn, so the turn is on the right leg, and turning to the left: the left knee is in passé. If the turn is to be a single turn, begin to step down and out of the turn with the left foot when only ¾ of the way around. This will prevent the momentum of the turn from causing the gymnast to overshoot the turn. If executing a double turn, step down after 1¾ turns of the rotation.

Sudden changes in direction add interest and an element of surprise. This is one of the aspects of jazz dancing that makes it so exciting and visually appealing. For example, the chassé with torso twist might be used as follows:

Side chassé: R.L.R. to counts 1 & 2. Arms open side and wrap (L. hand on right side of waist. R. arm bent and behind back). Focus is directed well over R. shoulder and down toward floor.

Step to L. on L., R. leg lifts to back attitude: Counts 3-4. Arms diagonally up and out, focus is up.

Execute ½ turn to R.: Bring R. leg to L., with feet parallel, and pivot to R. Count is 5; arms are still diagonally out and up; focus is out.

Sit and execute back extension: The sit is on count 6, back extension on 7-8.

What to watch for:

1. Chassé. Remember that it is with parallel feet. The left leg is straight (turned inside lunge), accent is downward on count of 2 with the right knee bent. The arms swing smoothly into the wrap position as everything moves: torso, head, focus and arms, all twist to the right.
2. Attitude. This is the contrast or element of surprise. The body should appear to dart into the movement and then suspend stretched fully upward for 2 counts. The change of direction is sharp and the focus moves from over the right shoulder to the left before any other movement occurs; the arms then reach upward to the V position (shoulders pulled down and fingers extended), while stepping into the back attitude position. The step is on the ball of the left foot with the knee straight and the hip bones lifted.
3. Half-pivot to left. From the attitude back, swing the right leg down to meet the left (parallel feet). Turn the head to the left to focus over the left shoulder just before beginning the pivot. Legs remain straight and torso well extended.

Pas de Bourre

Pas de bourre is another one of the basic steps frequently used in jazz dancing. It is generally executed in a parallel position of the feet with the knees slightly bent. The step may be performed traveling forward, alternating from side to side, turning, or remaining in place. Generally a connecting step or preparation for another move may be practiced while independently traveling forward. This movement, like so many other jazz steps, has an earthiness about it and should remain close to the ground. This does not mean, however, that the torso is not stretched.

Pas de bourre alternating and traveling forward:

Cross R. foot behind L.	open L. to side (2nd pos.)	step on R. to R. and slightly forward
1	&	2
Cross L. foot behind R.	open R. to side	step on L. to left
3	&	4

What to watch for:

1. Feet. The feet must remain completely parallel. There is a tendency to let them turn out slightly, particularly on a cross behind of the first step. A turning-out of the feet generally will weaken the line of a jazz movement. When the cross back of the first step is performed correctly, the right knee will appear tucked behind the left thigh.
2. Knees. Both knees remain slightly bent on all three steps of the pas de bourre. The head should not bob up and down with each step but remain level throughout the movement.
3. Weight transfer. Body weight remains centered and the feet step under or out from under the torso. In other words, there is no transfer of weight. This is the most difficult part of the movement to explain in words. To better understand the lack of any weight transfer, imagine a line down the center of the floor. Begin standing with the left foot on the line and the right foot off of the line to the right (parallel 2nd position). Cross the right foot behind the left so that it is just left of the line. Body weight is balanced over the imaginary line and between both feet. Without changing the weight of the body, place the left foot to the left of the line (about 12-14 inches). With the body weight still over the right leg, quickly pick up the right foot and place it just right of the line. The body will fall or drop onto the right foot while taking the 3rd step. It is almost as if the left foot were injured, forcing you to limp onto the right foot. As the movement is repeated from side to side, the torso will remain always over the imaginary line. When the step is actually performed, the transition should

be more smooth than this so that the gymnast does not appear to be hobbling down the floor.

Once the weight transfer has been successfully accomplished, add these arms to the movement:

- Begin parallel 2nd position with feet, arms extended side with palms down. Arms move to jazz first position as the right foot crosses back. Count 1.
- Arm moves forward (arm straight, palm down) and right arm opens side (arm straight, palm down). Count 2.

Continue in this fashion, traveling forward and alternating sides. Note that while the feet are moving 3 steps to 2 counts, the arms are moving 2 movements to 2 counts.

Ball Change Step or Catch Step

Two steps taken in any direction or in place to 1½ counts, with the second step being on the ball of the foot. The knees generally are slightly bent and the movement is rather subtle. The ball change step may also be used to change directions as in a pivot. The count for ball change step is "and 1," with the accent falling on the 2nd step. The first step is always on the ball of the foot, with the second step taking the accent.

PRACTICING KICKS ACROSS THE FLOOR

Control the torso. As the leg kicks forward, there should be a lengthening of the neck and spine, with the leg moving up to the chest, not the chest curving down toward the leg. Body weight transfers forward as the working leg swings up in front. Practice alternating kicks across the floor by stepping down into a slight lunge, weight over the forward leg, and swinging the opposite leg to kick. Practice holding the torso still, with hands extended side to jazz 2nd position, as you continue across the floor.

Variations

- straight support leg—straight kicking leg
- straight support leg, ball of foot—straight kicking leg
- bent support leg—straight kicking leg
- bent support leg with relevé—straight kicking leg

Adding an Arch or Lay-Back Position of the Torso to the Kick

1. Raise onto the ball of the support leg, on the upward swing of the leg, and just before it reaches maximum height, allow the torso to incline back. As the leg begins to come down, it pulls the body weight forward and the torso returns to upright position.
2. Kick the leg to its maximum height and as it begins to return to the ground, allow the body to arch back. After the foot returns to the floor, the torso straightens up.

All of the movements previously described are intended to serve only as a basis for understanding jazz movement; they allow the gymnast to experience the "manner" in which jazz is expressed through the body. These are only a few of the fundamental exercises and steps which comprise the dance form of jazz.

It is not suggested that the exercises in this chapter would ever be used independently in a floor or beam routine, but rather that one or more of these movements and body positions might be explored in combination with other steps, skills, or acrobatic moves. They are to be practiced in the repetitive form described only so that the gymnast may become more comfortable with the movement and achieve the control and coordination necessary, in much the same way that a particular tumbling skill is practiced.

9

Folk Dance

Traditionally, folk dancing was a celebration of important events in the community. These dances evolved naturally in conjunction with the everyday activities and experiences of the people who developed them. For example, the dances served to announce or celebrate various events such as festivals, courtships, weddings, the birth of a child, the planting of crops, and the harvest. Genuine folk dances are traditional dances; they are handed down from generation to generation and are more or less set in their basic pattern, although even traditional dances may vary slightly from region to region in the same manner as a basic language reveals different dialects.

Folk dances have a varied national heritage, rich in style and movement. Yet folk dances share a few basic steps common to various cultures. It is not necessary nor practical for the gymnast to adhere to any strict national flavor or pattern of folk dancing. Rather, the basic folk steps may be performed in the *manner* of the traditional dances, creating movements and variations of the basic steps which are more theatrical in their execution.

Folk dancing is a group or, at the very least, a couple or partner-type of dancing. As such, it is quite impossible for the gymnast to perform folk dancing in any genuine sense. One can only use folk dancing in its more theatrical manner, dancing the traditional folk steps and adding some ballet steps that can be performed with the "feel" or style of folk dancing. Since folk music is a frequent and desirable choice of music for the gymnast, some attention to it is given here.

The gymnast is completely free to combine folk steps in any way suitable. Certain body positions and methods of holding the arms will easily lend themselves

to these steps and help to describe a folk dance feeling; but remember that there is no right or wrong here, as what is performed is already a deviation from the original. It is the quality or essence of the original form that the gymnast should seek to preserve.

SOME EXAMPLES OF FOLK DANCE STEPS

Waltz Step: Balancé

Step forward on the R. foot, bending
  the R. knee. Legs are turned out.   count 1
Step with L. foot beside the R., rising onto the
  ball of the L. foot.   2
Step with R. foot in place and beside the L.
  (bend R. knee). Accent is on count 1 and   3
  the step is uneven. It may be danced from
  side-to-side, traveling forward, traveling
  back, or turning. In this case, the first
  waltz step would travel forward, the
  second waltz step would turn. For example:
Step forward with the R. foot, bending   count 1
  the R. knee.

Step forward with the L. foot, rising on the ball of the foot.	2
Step forward with the R. foot, bending the R. knee.	3
Step forward with the L. foot, bending the L. knee.	1
Step crossing behind L. foot with the R. (body turns R.).	2
Complete one full turn to the R. by stepping forward onto the L. foot.	3
You are now facing the direction from which you began.	

Pas de Basque

Step to the L. side with the L. foot (this is a light jump).	1
Touch R. toe across and in front of L. allowing weight to rest upon it briefly.	2
Step on L. foot in place	3

Movement may be done traveling forward or back. The accent is on count 1 and the rhythm is the same as the waltz step. The movement is large and sweeping and the hands are generally placed on the hips. The flavor of the Pas de basque may be altered by changing the first step to a jump and lifting the second leg up in a circular fashion before resting on it briefly. In this way the movement appears to begin with a slight hitch kick.

In any event, there is a twist at the waist as the torso remains forward while the hips turn on the diagonal with the cross step. This may be exaggerated still further by turning more in the waist and bringing the shoulders in opposition with the legs. As the left foot crosses the right foot, the right shoulder twists forward. The head is held high and the chest open.

Paddle Step (turning)

This is a pivoting step with the weight kept primarily over the leg that is pivoting.

Step down, onto the R. foot, bending the R. knee.	count 1
Step onto the L. foot as you place the ball of the L. foot beside the R.	and
Allow the body to turn ⅛ or ¼ to the R. as you step again onto the R. and in place.	2
Place the ball of the L. foot beside the R.	and

Allow the body to continue turning as
you step on the R. (The knees remain
relaxed and slightly turned-out. The
turn will not move off the spot the
gymnast is pivoting on and the body
will go up and down slightly with
each step. Arm positions are optional.)

Stamp

A forceful step made onto the entire foot, which may or may not involve a transfer
of weight. Feet are parallel and the legs together. The stamp is used as an accent
and may be performed with the supporting knee bent or straight.

Scuff

With the weight on the left leg, swing the right leg forward. The right knee is bent,
striking the right heel against the floor and into the air.

Step L., scuff R.   Step R., scuff L.   or
Step L., scuff R., hop L.   Step R., scuff L.   Hop R.

Heel and Toe

Touch the heel of one foot to the floor, forward and a little to the side, hopping
very slightly on the other foot. The toe of the same foot is then touched to the
floor across and in front of the other foot. There can be numerous variations and
patterns developed from the heel and toe step:

R. heel and toe.	count 1-2
L. heel and toe.	3-4
Touch L. toe to floor (knees turned in), slight hop on R.	5
Touch L. heel to floor (knees turned out), slight hop on R.	6
Stamp L. R. L.	7 and 8

Chug

Stand with weight on both feet. Instead of stepping forward on your right foot,
cause yourself to "fall" onto the foot. Immediately scoot the body weight forward
while remaining over the right foot and land flat footed on this same foot. This is
a "chug." The left leg may remain on the floor extended behind you as if you were
"dragging" the toe, or it may leave the ground as in a low arabesque.

The chug may be used independently within a group of steps; it may be used repetitiously as step right chug, chug, chug; or it may be used traveling and alternating legs, right chug, left chug.

Run

Movement of even rhythm with the weight transferring from one foot to another in a springing fashion: R. L. R. L. Feet are pointed and lifted behind while running.

Slide

A quick uneven step used to progress forward or side. The body is in the air most of the time and the feet make contact with the floor in a springing fashion.

Step forward with the R. foot.	count 1
Slide L. R. L. Slide R. L. R., alternately progressing forward	and a 2　and a 3

Or it may be performed in a series on one side only, while traveling forward or to the side. In ballet this step is known as chassé.

These are some of the traditional steps used in folk dancing; they are common to many nationalities and cultures. There are numerous steps within ballet which also are appropriate for use in a floor exercise routine where folk music is the choice. Some examples include balonné, assemblé, cabriole, jeté, pas de chat, and saute de chat.

STYLE

The essence of folk dancing is celebration. Keep in mind that the various dances marked an important event in the community and the style of the dancing reflects this. The movements are vibrant and robust, lively, colorful, and dramatic. This is characterized by large sweeping arm movements, lots of shouldering, and supplying an accent to the music through the use of a stamp, a change in the arms or shoulders, or a change in the position of the head.

In general, the women wore sturdy shoes and in some regions they wore boots. Consider this when reflecting on what the movement should look like. Dancing in boots lends itself very naturally to scuffing movements and stamping of the feet.

Positions of the Arms Which Reflect a Folk Style

1. Both hands on hips (back of the hand), elbows pressed forward.
2. Right arm extended over head, L. hand on hip. (Left shoulder pressed forward, R. shoulder pressed back, with the head turned toward the left and the chin lifted.)
3. Both arms folded across chest.
4. Figure eight movements of arms—crossing in front of the body independently or together.
5. Palm presses—bending the elbows and then straightening them as the heels of the hands are pressed directly to the sides, as if pushing a wall away from them on either side of the body.
6. Any large sweeping and circular movement of the arms. Starting with the arms extended to the sides, drop them down in front of the body, allowing them to cross as they are lifted in front and then over the head before opening to the side.

Example Combinations to Practice:

Example #1: Cabriole a la seconde (ka-bre-AWL) (ah la su-GAWND)

Step across right foot onto left, bending the left knee. Swing the right leg to your side (straight knee). Spring into the air, beating legs together at the ankle.

Figure 9.1 *Michele has landed on the left foot from the Cabriole.*

Land on the left leg in plié; right leg remains extended to the side. Legs are parallel and movement should travel sideways.

Step L.   cabriole to the R.   cabriole R.   (2 beats of the ankle)
   1 & 2   & 3
Balancé turning to your L., stepping R. L. R.
   4-5-6
Repeat

This step is performed traveling on a diagonal, with right hand on the hip, elbow pressed forward. Left hand is extended over head. The head is turned to the right on the cabrioles. Arms move to crossed position, figure eight fashion in front of chest on the balancé.

Example #2: Step on left foot and soutenue with the right as you complete one full rotation to the left. Transfer weight onto the right leg and bring the left leg immediately to passé and developpé to arabesque. Plié on the supporting leg.

Figure 9.2 *Michele shows the developpé back and plié on count 3 of the combination.*

Step L.	count 1
Cross R. over L. and turn L.	2
Developpé L. back and plié on R.	3
Arms describe a figure eight movement by crossing the chest on count 1 and opening side on count 3.	
Turn to the back leg and chassé L. R. L.	4
Tour jeté, kicking R.	5-6

10

The Balance Beam

When the gymnast moves from the floor to the balance beam, the rules and techniques of the various dance steps and movements remain the same. The approach to these movements, however, and the space in which the movements take place, vary dramatically. The width of the beam simply does not allow the feet to be fully turned-out. Unless the style of the movements requires a parallel position, the gymnast should still be instructed to work with the feet slightly turned-out so that proper alignment can be maintained, particularly on one leg balances. The tendency to align the foot with the beam while posing on one leg is most misguided. The look of the position is certainly less attractive and maintaining the pose is more difficult since the buttock muscles are generally not engaged here. Maximum turn-out or rotation of the legs must be reaffirmed in each of the dance movements as the leg or legs are extended off the beam.

On the beam, the carriage of the body, particularly the upper torso, the arms, and the focus, as well as the line of the body, takes on new importance. Dance steps are limited to one single line of travel; therefore the gymnast is heavily dependent on the full range of motion from both the legs and the arms so that the surrounding space may be used constructively. While on the floor, the gymnast is able to move about freely, creating various designs and patterns with movement. On the beam, the use of the arms becomes far more significant in creating interesting lines. The arms are an important factor in the dynamics of the routine, creating lyrical movements, accenting, framing the body, and changing the quality of the movements. The purpose of the arms as a tool for balance is more significant here as well.

The arm positions must remain controlled at all times and enhance the movements within the routine. There is nothing particularly interesting about arms that are in constant motion, arms that hang limply, or arms that remain in one position movement after movement. Much more consideration and training needs to go into the use of the arms during work on the beam routine. Encourage the gymnast to explore the different qualities of movement as well as the range of motion that the arms are capable of.

The following can be used to describe various qualities of the arm movements:

lyrical	pulsating
sharp	intertwined
dynamic	sweeping
controlled	expanding
sustained	percussive

Throughout the routine, the arms should reflect not one of these styles, but rather a variety of qualities by combining them with the movement of the legs or body to add interest to the routine. For example, consider how the movement for the arms can change the quality of a simple walking step where the arms move in opposition to the legs.

- *Percussive.* The arms move out sharply and stop suddenly in opposition to the walk. The arms will move just slightly before the legs so that they arrive at the same time as the step.
- *Sustained.* The arms swing downward with an accent and immediately out and up to waist height, sustaining the outward movement. (This is similar to a feeling of holding the breath.) In this instance, the arms accent downward as you step and lift to the sustained position as you "hold."

One can easily change the look of a movement simply by changing the arms, without ever changing the movement itself. Conversely, a lack of quality in the arms will leave the audience with a poor impression of the movement. There is little excuse for the arms to move repeatedly in the tried and true fashion when their range of movement and positions are seemingly endless.

The **range of motions** are:

- full circle
- half circle
- quarter circle

There are many, many circular arm pattern possibilities within this range of motions. Remember that the arms can move through these positions together, independently, or in opposition. They also may move horizontally, laterally, or diagonally through the circle.

Each individual has a personal inner time clock, a pace that is natural, as well as a quality of movement that is unique. When this timing and movement quality are combined with the potential range of motion, an individual's style and personality begin to emerge. Besides quality of movement and range of motion, we must also consider contrasting movement possibilities. These add interest to the routine and serve to make a statement to the movement or add an exclamation point to the visual image.

Movement Possibilities

- Sudden changes of direction
- Changes in levels
- Moving sideways on the beam as well as forward and back
- Independent movement of the wrist, head, foot, etc.
- Varying the counts of the movement

Despite the fact that there is no musical accompaniment for the beam work, it is helpful, nevertheless, to supply counts to the movements. This practice encourages syncopated movement and helps to prevent the monotony of moving evenly on a single beat. Keep in mind that it is not necessary to take a new position on every count.

For example, examine a simple arm swing:

1. Stand with feet together and arms crossed at the chest.
2. Swing both arms down and up to the right side, bending both elbows, with palms out. At the same time, bend both knees and turn head to the R.

Swing down.	count 1
Swing up to R. side.	
Bend the knees and turn the head.	2

Now alter the swing so that as the arms come up to the right side, you sharply pulse the finger tips back two times by bending the hand at the wrist.

Swing arms down and up to the R.	count 1
Pulse fingers back two times (from wrist).	"and" 2
Turn head to right.	3
Bend knees.	4

Quite often a single movement of the wrist or head will add color to an otherwise monotonous movement.

The following two examples show how easily alterations can be made in a single movement that will expand the movement possibilities for the gymnast. In both examples, the gymnast is moving from a forward lunge position to a scale in 4 counts.

Begin in lunge position, holding the pose.	counts 1-2
Contract body (lifting back leg to chest).	3
Extend lifted leg to scale-flat back position (one straight line from fingers to foot parallel to beam).	4

In this example the accent is on count 3 with a sharp pull inward of the arms and knee, followed by a sharp extension of the leg to the scale, with the arms stretched forward. The movement is dynamic in quality, showing contrast and syncopation.

In the following example, the movement is lyrical in quality, the counts are even, and the movement is much smoother and more understated.

Begin in the lunge position and hold pose.	count 1
Circle upper torso and arms to side, back, and then side, finishing with arms extended to the sides (horizontal).	2
Bring back leg to passé position turned out—arms close to 1st position.	3
Extend leg to scale—change arms to 1st position arabesque.	4

Explore other methods of transition from a lunge to a scale pose by changing:

arm positions
levels of the lunge or scale
counts of the movement

As you can see, by exploring and embellishing one movement, the gymnast can create endless possibilities to enhance her routine, adding interest and variety.

IMPROVISATION

On the balance beam, where the working space of the gymnast is greatly restricted, creating interesting pictures with the body becomes very important. Improvisation is one method for exploring this potential. The following exercises are offered to show how effective improvisation can be when used as a method for exploring potential movements on the beam routine.

Exercise 1

Stand on one leg. Explore various levels of space and body positions while remaining on one leg. Supply counts to the movements; show contrast and changes in quality while moving from one position to another. Include in the movement changes of focus, arms, legs, and torso. Experiment with different images that may change the interpretation of the movement.

For example, imagine catching a balloon floating by. Relate to its roundness by moving the body or arms in complementary and harmonious fashion. Then release the balloon into the air. This may be done with the hands, the knee, foot, etc. Practice the movement until it is more refined and less literal. If you chose to release the balloon by kicking with the knee, this might become a contraction of the torso; arms to knee, knee turned-in passé position, and supporting leg bent. This is then followed by an extension of the raised leg to arabesque, lifting and arching the torso and opening the arms over head while rising onto the ball of the standing foot. From the extended position, fall forward into a lunge (arabesque leg swings forward to lunge). Supply 6 or 8 counts to the refined movement of catching and releasing the balloon. Now insert the movement pattern into the middle of a pass across the beam.

Another example: Back walkover to handstand, one leg through to split sit, swing one leg forward to stand. Insert movement pattern, then move from lunge into a split leap.

Exercise 2

Imagine a sudden, loud clapping noise that comes from above. Respond by covering the head with your arms. Wait a moment and then tentatively extend one arm over the head to investigate; then extend the second arm and finally gather the courage to look upward. Annoyed at being startled over nothing, aggressively and courageously strike out at the space around you.

This movement might be refined to become a sudden, slight bend in the knees and spinal twist to the left, with focus down and arms bent at the elbows and crossed over head. Hold position for one or two counts. Leaving the focus down and the torso twisted to the left, press right arm upward to the ceiling, fingers extended, palm facing up to the ceiling and heel of the hand leading the movement. Lift the focus and spiral the torso upward out of the twist as the left hand presses to the ceiling in the same fashion. As you extend the chest and torso still further, circle the arms out to the side and down while stepping forward onto the right foot. Then brush the left foot forward, taking the arms overhead as you execute a fouetté turn to the right over the left to pose with one arm extended upward and the other beside the legs, reaching down.

Encourage the gymnasts to create little, personal scenarios, refining the movement so that it becomes less literal. Let them experiment with movements that depict different emotions, sound levels, and intensities, enabling them to devise their own unique movements, thus tapping their own creativity.

Once the skills that the gymnast is going to perform are decided upon, then the previously described methods may be used to add color, flavor, and style to the routine. It is most important that the gymnast's personality is able to emerge during the presentation. This creates the style and gives the gymnast a vehicle for expressing something that is uniquely her own.

Presentation of movement should come from within. In this way it is explored and expressed through every part of the body. Each movement should have a relationship to the previous movement, regardless of whether it flows smoothly from one to the other or is sharply disconnected. There must always be a sense of continuity to the routine and it should never appear to be just a collection of unrelated movements and skills. Every part of the body is important, with all movements being an extension from one's "center" or inner focus that is directed to even the very tips of the fingers. Instruct the gymnast to feel this energy throughout the body, so she can develop a sense and awareness of where the body is in space and what it is doing. Too often the gymnast directs her total concentration exclusively on the execution of a specific skill without realizing that her fist has clenched, her elbow has drooped, or her foot has become flexed unattractively.

If the gymnast is encouraged to feel the movement coming from within, the movements will look less like some heavy outer garment lying on top of the body and weighing it down.

When choreographing or putting together a competitive beam routine, we can classify the routine into three distinct areas:

1. The skills (required leaps, gymnastic skills, turns, etc.). These are determined by the abilities and skill level of the gymnast.
2. The icing (those balances and movements that come from improvisation and express the individual style of the gymnast as well as adding interest and variety to movement). The previously described improvisational exercises should be helpful in adding insight and dimension to this aspect of the routine.
3. The connecting dance steps. The following are a list of dance steps appropriate for work on the beam:
   assemblé (ah-sahm-BLAY)
   assemblé battu (ba-TEW)
   cabriole (ka-bre-AWL) front or back
   chassé (sha-SAY)

jeté (zhuh-TAY)
pas de cheval (pas-duh-shuh-VAL)
sauté (soh-TAY)
sissonne changé (shahn-ZHAY)
ballonné (ba-low-NAY)
changement (shahnzh-MAHN)
fouetté (feweh-TAY)
tour jeté
royale (rwah-YAL)
sissonne (see-SAWH) open and closed
soubresaut (soo-bruh-SOH)

Note that a sissonne changé is executed in the prescribed manner but with a change of the legs while in the air. If you begin the movement with the right foot in front, the legs will switch immediately following take-off so that you land forward on the left foot, closing the right foot in back.

Here are some further considerations for the form and structure of the movement when putting together a beam routine:

- contrasting movement (tension-relaxation)
- changes in direction, level, size, and shape of the movement
- rhythmic patterns (even and uneven)
- variations in use of energy (accent, quality, intensity)

Finally, be discriminating. Observe the overall routine with an objective eye. Don't be afraid to make changes if the routine does not seem to flow well or if a certain movement does not seem to fit the gymnast. Once a particular movement has been put together, scrutinize that movement carefully and avoid letting the arms move about aimlessly.
Here is a checklist of pitfalls to watch for:

1. filling space with *any* movement
2. too much or not enough contrast
3. does the movement enhance the routine or is it just filling space?
4. does the movement look good on this particular gymnast?
5. lack of continuity
6. devoid of *any* style

LEARNING TO DANCE ON THE BALANCE BEAM

Just as the gymnast must repeatedly practice acrobatic and tumbling movements, she must also give thorough concentration to dance movements on the beam. It is critical that the gymnast displays complete confidence and control during the beam presentation, both with dance movements and gymnastic skills. The only way of accomplishing this and acquiring an understanding of how to handle the body during the dance movements is to progressively study the movement on the beam.

First work with one movement at a time, instructing the gymnast to do the movement repetitively as well as in a series, working up and down the beam. Instruct the gymnast to also apply specific arm positions to the movement. The positions chosen are irrelevant; the point is that the gymnast must be able to maintain a given arm position while focusing exclusively on the legs and maintaining balance on the beam. It is paramount that the kinesthetic sense, or muscle memory, be developed so that the gymnast is able to consistently find proper alignment in dance steps as easily as she does with gymnastic skills. Just as a tight pulled-up body and pointed feet need to become automatic in a handstand, so must the awareness of what even the fingertips are doing become automatic in a dance movement. The gymnast does not have time to think of each aspect of a movement independently. It must all come together at one time. There is no magic to accomplishing this, it is simply a matter of practice and learning the movements in a progressive fashion. After an individual movement has been carefully studied and performed in a series with changes in the arm movements, progress to combining two or more steps together. Slowly work in this fashion, gradually changing and adding movement, until more complicated combinations are being worked.

Do not be any less demanding of the dance movements on the beam than you are of the gymnastic skills. The gymnast knows that it is not enough to just be able to stay on the beam when doing a cartwheel, for example. It is clearly understood that a cartwheel is not satisfactory unless it is also performed with straight legs, pointed toes, etc. The same is true of a pirouette. Staying on the beam is simply not enough; it only means that the gymnast has successfully learned how to spin on one leg without falling off. This is not a pirouette.

To help the gymnast become more aware of the arms and hands, suggest practicing movement up and down the beam while holding onto a round ball. Urge experimenting with circular movement while holding the ball, engaging the spine and the focus as well as exploring lateral movement of the arms. Practice holding two smaller balls, one in each hand and experimenting with independent movement of the arms.

MOVEMENT COMBINATIONS TO PRACTICE ON THE BALANCE BEAM

The following examples are offered as a guide to show the manner in which dance steps or movement phrases may be taught and practiced. The specific steps should first be practiced independently as skills, then integrated into movement phrases so that the gymnast may become more proficient at movement across the beam. Practicing movement phrases on the beam helps the gymnast to develop style and smooth out transitions and promotes performing with confidence and fluidity.

Table 10.1 *Chassé*

The Movement	Arm Position	What To Watch For
Perform in a series, beginning first with the R. leg leading. Also practice: Repetitive chassés with L. leg leading. Movement should be practiced until the gymnast can move quickly across the beam with no hesitation between the chassés.	2nd pos. arabesque (arm opposition to legs). Arms extended to the side (lateral-palms down, wrist slightly lifted).	The hand of the forward arm stays in line with the center of the body. Forward arm lifted chest height but low enough so that the focus may be directed over the hand. Hands should not hang limply from the break at the wrist but should feel like an extension out to the finger tips. The position of the arms in relationship to the body should not change as the chassé is performed. They should not be seen bobbing about but held firmly in place. Shoulders held down and chest lifted. Long neck. The foot steps onto the beam, toe, ball, heel. There is a slight and smooth plié on the forward leg as weight is transferred forward just before the lift into the air. Both legs are straight and crossed in sous-sus position while in the air. The landing should be smooth. The plié should not jolt the body and movement impulse of the chassé is in a continuous forward fashion. Feet are well pointed throughout, legs straight and turned-out as much as the beam allows.

Table 10.2 *Directional Changes and the Fouetté*

The Movement	Arm Position	What To Watch For
Walk forward with 4 steps (R. L. R. L.). Swing the R. leg forward to fouetté and pivot ½ around to L. leg. R. leg is now in back. Walk backwards 4 steps (R. L. R. L.). Swing R. leg back to fouetté, pivoting on the L. and turning ½ around to the R. to face front. R. leg is now extended forward. Practice the movement reversing the walks and the fouettés. Maintain a strong upward pull of the waist line during the fouettés to prevent any bobbles in the upper torso.	No arms.	Legs are well stretched—stepping toe, ball, heel—on the walks. Focus will lead the directional change on the fouetté. Torso must extend strongly up and slightly forward as it turns into the first fouetté so that there is room for the leg to turn over in the socket. The extension of the torso must come from lifting the abdominal muscles. The heel of the supporting leg must move forward on the fouetté. This is accomplished by maintaining the connection in the buttocks and applying inward pressure to the ankle. The established height of the leg as it is brushed forward is maintained during the fouetté. Do not allow it to drop as it turns over. To fouetté from back to front, the hip of the working leg must pull back toward the supporting leg as it turns over in the socket. The established height of the leg must be maintained or lifted higher but will not drop as the leg rotates from the backward position to a forward position. Torso must get taller not shorter as the leg flips over. Both fouettés must pivot on the ball of the supporting foot.

Table 10.3 *Step Jeté*

The Movement	Arm Position	What To Watch For
This is performed as a small leap, stepping down on the L. foot and immediately leap onto the R. (stride leap). The movement is performed as in a series with no stops between the leap and the following step. The movement is not large but a certain amount of elevation and speed are required. Movement should be practiced with the R. and L. leaps regardless of the gymnast's handedness.	Opposition to the leg. 1st position on preparatory step and move to 2nd position arabesque on the jeté, or hands may be held in lateral position throughout the step and the leap.	The preparatory step is onto a small plié. Foot steps toe, ball, heel. The extension of the arms into the desired position and the brush of the leg into the leap are simultaneous. As the leg moves forward into the stride position, there must be a strong push from the supporting leg. The brush and the push are almost simultaneous, with the push following only an instant behind. Too much pause between the brush and the push will interrupt the flow of the movement. As the front foot lands from the leap, immediately bring the back leg forward for the preparatory step of the next leap. Be sure that there is a strong abdominal pull upwards and a lift of the hip bones so that the body does not rock in the air. Do not lift from the shoulders. Both legs should be fully stretched in the air. Toes are pointed. Instruct the gymnast to be aware of the arms and hands all the way to the tips of the fingers. The movement impulse of the step jeté is in a continuous forward fashion with no hesitation between the step, the jeté, or the following step.

Table 10.4 *Ballonné*

The Movement	Arm Position	What To Watch For
Step L., ballonné R. ballonné R.	4th position arms (L. arm forward).	Step forward onto a small plié on the L. foot, with hip bones lifted so that the pelvis does not "sit" backward.
Step R., ballonné L.	4th position arms (R. arm forward).	The brush into the ballonné is with a well stretched leg and pointed toe to the height of about 45°. Spring off of the L. leg and slightly forward to meet the R. as the R. foot comes to coupé position at the ankle of the L. leg. The landing of the L. and the coupé position of the R. are simultaneous. Although the ballonné should appear to be a light, springy movement, the emphasis will be *in* on the landing. The count is: "and" one. The foot of the brushing leg meets the ankle of the pushing foot by virtue of a strong inward pull of the foot to coupé position. There is a slight twist in the waist in opposition to the forward leg, and the body inclines forward slightly.
There should be no stop between the ballonnés. Remember that ballonné means "bounced" and the momentum should smoothly carry the gymnast from the first ballonné into the second.		

Table 10.5 *Assemblé and Sissonne*

The Movement	*Arm Position*	*What To Watch For*
Step forward on the L. ft. into a small plié. Assemblé with R. leg (swings forward and lands on both feet).	Arms down at sides. Arms swing freely up and out to a diagonally lifted position and drop slightly down on the landing.	The first step down is a preparatory step and the weight transfers this leg so that it propels upward with a strong push of the foot into the assemblé. The brushing leg should swing up to 90° height. The push off of the supporting leg is almost simultaneous with the brush and only slightly after. The brushing leg must quickly move back down and under the torso so that the feet land at the same time in a small plié. Keep the hip bones lifted on the landing so that the pelvis does not "sit" backward. The assemblés should travel slightly forward.
Sissonne open travels forward (lands in arabesque on the R. in plié). Repeat this movement phrase across the beam pausing only between complete phrases. Movement should be repeated and practiced on the reverse side. Movement should be smooth and lyrical with each movement connected to the previous one and the sissonne being the largest movement with the most emphasis. Use two complete phrases to cross the beam one time.	Arms lift to 2nd position arabesque (opposition to the legs) on the sissonne.	The sissonne should immediately follow the landing of the assemblé with no noticeable pause. Be sure that the forward arm when in 2nd arabesque is not beside the head but in front of the chest and centered with the focus directed over the hand. The base leg of the sissonne must propel forward almost as in a split action.

Table 10.6 *Waltz Count Combination*

The Movement	Arm Position	What To Watch For
Perform to a 3 count as in a waltz.		
Count 1 Step forward onto the R. foot	Arms down at sides.	
Count 2-3 Grand battement forward with L. leg	Lift to 2nd position arabesque (R. arm forward, L. back).	Torso should appear to lift and get taller as leg kicks up. This is a smooth lift of the leg. Foot pointed and both legs straight.
Count 1-2 Spring forward onto the L. foot (bending knee). At the same time, R. foot moves to parallel coupé (R. foot to L. ankle).	Both arms cross to R. diagonally down and back.	Clearly show the coupé position at side of ankle.
Count 3 Lift R. foot to side of L. knee, which is still parallel (parallel retire position). Head dropped backward.		Clearly show retiré position. Supporting knees are still bent but torso is well extended. No curved back.
Count 1 Step forward on ball of R.	Arms down.	Legs are fully stretched and abdominals well lifted with the buttock muscles engaged. Torso is lifted up and out away from the legs.
Count 2 Step forward on ball of L.		
Count 3 Step back on ball of R.		
Count 1 Quick pivot and ½ turn to R.	Slight lift and spiral of arms to the R.	Shoulders remain over the hips during the ½ turn and the torso moves in one unit. To pivot, apply inward pressure to ankles and heels. Keep a tight body and initiate the pivot by spotting first over R. shoulder, then over L. to return.
Count 2 Quick pivot and ½ turn to L.		
Count 3 Drop into plié on L., with R. foot to parallel coupé at side of L. ankle.	Both arms diagonally down and back to R., with focus over R. shoulder.	

160

11

Dance Injuries and
Their Prevention

This chapter does not examine the structural deformities or various body types that may contribute to a particular injury. Such physical problems as curvature of the spine, knock knees, flat feet, etc., present very special problems for the gymnast and her coach that are beyond the scope of this book. Indeed, it is questionable whether a gymnast who exhibits any of these deformities should be accepted into a competitive program. While the therapeutic benefits of various physical activities like dance and gymnastics cannot be disputed, in a program with a demanding competitive team schedule it would be difficult to give the gymnast the special attention these kinds of physical problems require. The physical stress placed on the body by gymnastics is great and the body types of potential gymnasts should be closely scrutinized before the student is accepted into a competitive program.

This chapter will confine itself strictly to an overview of injuries that are likely to arise from faulty technique. It also will present conditioning or strength building exercises for the development of specific muscles that in a weakened state may contribute to a chronic strain or injury.

CHRONIC STRAINS

The most effective safeguard for preventing injury is correct execution. Many injuries are actually the result of faulty technique. This can be the case even when

the cause of the injury appears to be a sudden isolated incident such as a twisted ankle or unexpected tearing of a leg muscle. The catalyst for the subsequent injury may actually have been an accumulation of wear and tear to the strained area due to poor positioning. The muscle or joint finally gives way when conditions are right; the excitement of a meet, a late night out before practice, or exhaustion due to a heavy workload. If an error in technique is involved, it is probable that once the gymnast returns to her training schedule, the injury will reoccur or resurface in the form of a chronic strain. This should be the signal that she is working in a manner that makes her susceptible to that particular weakness.

Pains that develop gradually over a period of time with no obvious catalyst, such as a fall, occur when a specific part of the body is receiving constant irritation, producing inflammation of the corresponding tissue. A chronic condition or reoccuring injury can also be the result of weak or atrophied muscles that fail to do their job in supporting the body through a specific movement. If the gymnast begins to complain of a pain of an ambiguous origin, watch her body placement while executing movements that strain the painful area.

BODY CONDITIONING

The more closely the physique of the gymnast conforms to the ideal and is free of structural problems, the less opportunity there is for injury. Even with a good physique, an integrated program that strengthens all of the muscles of the body is an important part of the gymnast's conditioning. It has been my experience that too frequently, training programs simply build on the natural strengths and weaknesses of the gymnast. The student with strong thighs and weak calves, for example, will continue to work in a fashion that compensates for that particular muscle inequity; that is, the thigh muscles continue to do more of the work, getting stronger and stronger, while the calf muscles deteriorate further as they do less and less.

Dance is a skill of total body movement. Since dance requires coordination of various muscular groups, complete muscular development is preferable over strengthening specific muscles. Conditioning is recommended as an adjunct to the gymnast's training and a program that incorporates strengthening exercises that complement dance movements will be the most beneficial. These exercises should strengthen muscles without interfering with flexibility. This is accomplished by including exercises that stretch the body at the point of initiation. Examples of exercises that are useful in body conditioning are included at the end of this chapter. In many cases, the exercises are the same as those used in the rehabilitation of a muscle following an injury. This suggests that if the muscle had been properly strengthened at the onset, injury might have been avoided.

WARM-UP

Professional dancers, athletes, sports medical specialists, and coaches sometimes hold conflicting opinions as to the type of warm-up necessary to prepare the body to move, but all would agree that some type of warm-up is needed for most activities. There are many elements to consider in setting up your own warm-up program. The age of your gymnasts, length and structure of work out, the weather, if it is the middle or beginning of the competitive season—these are all factors to be evaluated. The length of time spent on the warm-up is less crucial than the method used for warming up. One cannot ignore the connection between injury and lack of warm-up when a gymnast suffers torn muscles or ligaments while attempting her first split leap during workout.

The purpose of any warm-up is to prepare the muscles to move; to put the muscles through the full range of flexibility required of them in the following activity; and to prepare the muscles for an increased output of strength. To adequately warm the muscles so that they are more pliable, the body temperature must be raised. A warmer body, in turn, increases the blood flow to the muscles, which produces the heat necessary for safely stretching the body. Note that passive methods for warming the muscles, such as massage, deep heat creams, and hot showers, are ineffectual. Also note that although the use of leg warmers and body suits are somewhat helpful in retaining body heat, particularly in a cold gym, their use is an inadequate substitute for body heat that is generated by muscular activity.

Stretching exercises that prepare the gymnast for her flexibility requirements should be included in the warm-up. However, any serious stretching, designed for increasing the gymnast's range of flexibility, should not be encouraged until the end of the workout session. Stretching the muscles and improving flexibility can be accomplished by three different methods: ballistic stretching (bouncing), static stretching, and resistance stretching. The ballistic method of stretching is no longer looked upon with much favor by most professionals and should be avoided. This technique of using the pull of gravity and the weight of the body in a bobbing fashion to force a particular stretch is actually tearing muscle fiber with each bounce and can result in muscle or tendon injury. Consequently, the controlled or static stretch is generally considered to be more satisfactory. This requires that the body be pulled smoothly into the maximum stretched position. The body is held here for several seconds, after which all air is forced out of the lungs with a deep exhalation, allowing the body to relax still further. As the air is exhaled, the body is gently pulled further into the stretched position. This type of stretching is quite effective and generally improves the range of flexibility.

The third technique for stretching, resistance stretching, is a popular method of increasing flexibility among dancers and gymnasts. This type of stretching requires a partner and involves the contraction of one muscle group followed by the stretching of the same muscle group. For example, to stretch the inner thigh muscles, one gymnast sits on the floor in a straddle position with the body rounded forward. The second gymnast stands behind her partner and applies downward pressure to the back while the first gymnast resists by attempting to lift the back against this pressure, holding the position for several seconds before releasing. This is followed with a stretching of the muscles by attempting to pull the body to the floor as far as possible without the aid of the partner. The gymnasts should repeat this process five times. This stretching method can be used in various other positions. For example, sitting on the floor, with soles of the feet together, and knees open, lift knees and contract muscles against downward pressure from partner. Or sit with legs extended forward in pike position, body relaxed over legs, and lift the back upward against downward pressure from a partner. A third example involves standing with your back to the wall, one leg raised toward the shoulder, and contracting muscles while pulling the leg down against upward pressure from a partner. Or face the wall with one leg raised into arabesque and pull the leg down against resistance offered by partner who is attempting to lift the leg up. Although the technique of resistance stretching is quite effective, it is not recommended for young gymnasts because a certain amount of maturity and body awareness is required on the part of the gymnast who is offering the resistance. In each example given, the gymnast offering resistance must stop applying pressure before the gymnast being stretched stops contraction of the muscle.

Another important aspect to warming-up is balancing the muscle groups being worked. A contraction of one muscle group requires an equal pull or elongation of the opposite muscle group. A contraction of the quadricep muscle on the front of the leg for example, requires the stretch of the hamstring muscle at the back of the leg. When one muscle group is stronger than the other, the weaker muscle, or the joint the muscle protects, becomes prone to injury. Keeping this in mind, any stretching of the hamstring muscle should be followed with exercises that contract that same muscle group; any back bending of the thorax and lumbar region must be followed with exercises that stretch those areas of the spine.

So far we have focused on the physical benefits of the warm-up session. Keep in mind that the mental benefits of the warm-up are equally important in preparing the gymnast to move, in preventing injury, and in insuring a productive workout session. The warm-up is the transition state between the normal physical and mental state and the workout or athletic state. Breathing exercises serve to prepare the gymnast for her workout by calming the mind and body, increasing body aware-ness, and allowing her to focus inward, all of which produces a psychological readiness.

The warm-up session should begin with the gymnast standing, with feet com-fortably apart, and arms down at sides. Instruct the gymnast to inhale deeply, breathing through the nose and feeling the energy rising up from the base of the spine and out the top of the head as the arms extend to the sides of the body and over the head. Exhale slowly, pressing the shoulder blades down toward the waist as the arms lower to the sides of the body and the spine continues to elongate while resisting the downward pressure of the arms. This should be repeated several times and followed by head rolls, performed slowly to one side and then to the other. Next, move on to waist and leg stretches before beginning the cardiovascular or aerobic part of the workout. This could be jogging around the room, stationary aerobic exercises involving fast arm circles, calisthenics such as jumping jacks, or choreographed fast-paced dance steps. The warm-up section of the workout should always conclude with stretching exercises to release calf muscles contracted during the aerobic section as well as stretches that work the flexibility range required of gymnastics, i.e., splits and arches. Lastly, conditioning exercises should be given that strengthen the entire musculature of the body. Keep in mind that the gymnast should always conclude her session with some of the same stretches and condi-tioning exercises that were performed during the warm-up.

There are many considerations in personalizing your warm-up session. Time allotment is certainly one of the more significant factors and a minimum of 10 minutes should be given to warming up, with 20 minutes being preferable. The body must be adequately prepared through a thorough warm-up that increases the heart rate, raises the deep temperatures within the body, and stretches the muscles, tendons, and ligaments if it is to withstand the aggressive physical activity of gymnastics.

THE FEET

In all weight bearing movements, the feet must firmly support the body by pressing equally into the ground at three points: in front through the ball of the foot; at the heads of the 1st and 5th metatarsal; and in back at the heel. This triangular base gives support to the muscles of the leg and feet and allows the muscles to work correctly in support of the arch. This base should be functional at all times so that even in a pointed position the foot is felt to pull equally from the heel upward toward the calf and from the ankle through the 1st and 5th toes. By feeling an equal contraction of the heel to the calf and a lengthening of the foot through the toes, any rolling in of the foot is prevented. The act of propulsion is performed by the toes, in particular the large toe, which is the strongest, and any rolling in will ultimately affect the strength of the ankle joint and inhibit the strong push-off so necessary to the gymnast in leaps and tours. Gymnasts should be observed closely, early in their training, to insure that the muscles of the feet are functioning properly and that any strain or stress to the ankles is kept to a minimum.

When the leg is straight it is aligned in a vertical position over the foot and at a right angle to the foot. This is the natural alignment and is maintained in a turned-out position as well, by rotating the leg at the hip and maintaining the triangular base at the foot, firmly feeling the 3 points of balance pressing into the floor. It becomes increasingly difficult to achieve this alignment as the student works for greater and greater turn-out, but the importance of seeing that the gymnast does not over rotate at the ankle in her effort to achieve turn-out cannot be overstated. Over rotating will result in abduction of the forefoot and subsequently weaken the whole musculature of the foot. If turn-out initiates from the knees or ankles rather than the hip area, the correct alignment of the leg is destroyed and the inner side of the foot rolls inward, disrupting the proper weight bearing distribution. This rolling inward can lead to irreversible overstretching of the ligaments and also can contribute to achilles tendonitis. Equally disconcerting is the overcompensation that may take place when the gymnast shifts her weight to the outer edge of the foot, leading to strain in the arch. By maintaining a stable ankle position while correctly turning out at the hip, and by including strengthening ankle and foot exercises in the workout, proper weight bearing should be achieved.

Pain Along the Inside of the Foot

If the gymnast has been made aware of a tendency to "falling" on the foot, but is experiencing a pain along the inside of the foot, it is likely to be a result of her effort to control the "roll." Persistent pain indicates that the ligaments are feeling the strain of the adjustment. Ligaments are quicker to react and slower to recover from strains during workout than muscles are.

Joint Pain in the Toes

Joint pain, particularly in the large toe, is generally the result of one or two bad habits. One bad habit is curling the toes under to achieve the appearance of a high arch in the pointed foot. When pointing the foot, the gymnast should think of contracting the heel upward toward the calf, while at the same time extending the toes, lengthening them away from the ankle. This in itself will develop a strong foot that is less susceptible to injury. The other poor habit that may result in chronic pain is pressing the big toe or "stubbing" the toe into the floor while the leg is extended to a pointed position on the floor. This is seen frequently on beam work when the gymnast assumes a posed position and uses the pointed toes for balance. The gymnast should never allow her body weight to rest on the pointed toe.

KNEES

Correct alignment of the knee in relationship to the thigh and leg will rarely result in any strain. In most injuries, the problem arises from improper positioning of the leg while in a bent knee position.

Although this chapter does not discuss structural problems that give rise to injury, an exception will be made regarding the hyperextension of the knee joint. This condition exists if the leg, when observed from the side, appears as a slight semi-circle rather than at the right angle to the foot, which is typical of the normal leg. This hyperextension is present when the muscles and ligaments over the front and back of the knee are over stretched. Body weight distribution here is a problem as most of the weight will fall back on the heels, thus interfering with the ability to achieve satisfactory elevation. The gymnast with this condition is highly susceptible to pain, just above or below the patella (knee cap). The "swayback" position of the joint makes pulling up the thigh muscles dangerous. If the muscles of the knee are contracted too forcibly or the knee joint is "locked" into position or "jammed" in an effort to straighten and tighten the leg, pain is likely to result. This particular structural problem needs careful attention during the early training of the gymnast so that permanent damage is not done to the knee. Even the gymnast without hyperextended knees can experience pain slightly above or below the patella if there is a tendency toward over zealous tightening or pulling up of the thigh muscles while in a standing position.

The knee joint is primarily capable of only hinge-like movement. A very small amount of side-to-side rotation is possible, but then only when the knee is bent and only when the knee is *not* in a weight bearing position. Consequently, any inward or outward falling of the knee out of alignment with the thigh and ankle while in a weight bearing position will likely result in strain to the knee.

This brings us to the plié, the first exercise performed in the ballet class. Pliés, even when executed correctly and with perfect alignment, can be taxing for the knees and are of some controversy among dancers. While it is true that the gymnast does not begin her workout with demi and grand pliés at the barre as the dancer does, she still must understand the correct placement and use of the legs in plié as it is an important transition in many dance steps. The plié also serves as an important shock absorber in the landing from all movements of elevation. While the gymnast may never execute the traditional plié of the ballet dancer, she certainly will perform movements and poses that pass through a bent knee position. With this in mind, remember that any time the body is in a weight bearing position with one or both legs bent, the knee must lie directly over the foot and toes with the knee and thigh neither rolling inward or outward of the ankle. Always remember that turn-out is initiated from the hip joint, not from the knee or ankle.

Bursae are sacks of fluid in the vicinity of the knee which serve to prevent friction and cushion against pressure or blows to the knee area. Kneeling on the beam or repeated knee falls in a floor routine can contribute to painful knee conditions resulting from inflammation of the bursae. If the gymnast is suffering from this condition, knee pads should be worn in practice to keep the irritation at a minimum. Once the bursae is inflamed, the gymnast may find that even complete extension of the leg, such as in arabesque, is difficult.

In general, any ballistic type of stretching that involves the knees should be used sparingly due to the strain that it puts on the ligaments and bursae of the knee area.

HIP STRAIN

Mobility and rotation in the hip joint are essential for the extensions and amplitude required in movements of the legs, such as splits and split leaps. This mobility is made possible by the numerous muscles, tendons, and ligaments that attach and cross from the last vertebrae of the spine to the hip joint, making the relationship of the pelvis to the back and thigh important. In the gymnast's zeal to increase her forward and middles splits, groin muscles that have failed to acquire the necessary muscle tone are commonly overstretched. Muscular strength of the hip and inner thigh need to be increased proportionately with any gain in joint flexibility.

Even well-conditioned groin muscles are susceptible to strain when movements are executed with the pelvis out of alignment. If the pelvis is pressed too far backward while the legs are turned out, the result will be a hollowing of the low back and undo pressure on the knees and ankles. Conversely, tucking the pelvis forward while rotating the legs outward places the ligaments in a dangerous position, particularly in movements that elevate the leg to the front or side. Persistent groin strain will likely be the result of this poor placement. Remember that the position of the pelvis in relationship to the spine and knees is far more important than the amount of turn-out achieved in the hip socket. Strain in the groin area may appear on the inner or forward part of the hip, or along the outside of the thigh. The pain is most noticeable when the leg is lifted to the front or side position. A deeper strain will be apparent in nonweight bearing positions and when the legs are elevated or stretched, say, in a straddle sit position. Despite the beauty of a flexible hip movement requiring extension of the leg, it is not wise for the gymnast to work for this flexibility if sufficient muscular strength does not accompany the stretch.

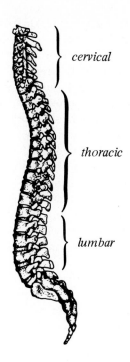

cervical

thoracic

lumbar

THE BACK

The muscularly weak lower back is highly susceptible to stress, so stretching exercises for the lower back and strengthening exercises for the abdominals are recommended.

There are two categories of injuries to the spine, the more serious being disc-related problems. The intervertebral discs are insensitive to pain, and it is actually the nearby nerve roots responding to pressure from stressful activity and overstretching of ligaments that signal pain. The discs serve as a type of shock absorber and, over time, are subject to some degeneration from wear and tear, the extent of which is predisposed by the individual's constitution as well as the extent of trauma endured and the type of condition which results from a slit in the posterior "arc" segment of a vertebra body. This problem requires the immediate attention of a physician specializing in these problems.

Most sprains of the back are less serious and will respond to rest and heat or cold, specific exercises, massage, or ultrasound treatment. In cases of muscle spasms, ice combined with gradual stretching of the afflicted area will relieve the symptoms quickly. As with any other part of the body, prevention through appropriate conditioning and correct technique is invaluable to the longevity of the gymnast's career.

It is generally accepted that the human spine is in the process of evolutionary change and that this contributes to the great diversity in how backs are formed. For example, some individuals have four and even six lumbar vertebrae instead of five. This, along with posture, body alignment, and the attempts by the gymnast to exceed the normal structural limitations of the spine, can contribute to serious injuries. Constantly seeking to improve technique and understanding of correct alignment are crucial in avoiding potential problems in this area.

Arabesque is a frequent source of back problems. Pain results from hyper-extension of the back or failure to keep the pelvis level. The proper arabesque should spread the extension throughout the entire spine rather than forcing the movement at the bottom in the lower back.

Another contributor to back strain is improper warm-up followed by sudden rotation or hyperextension of the spine. In beginning students, a susceptibility to lower back strain is often associated with weak abdominals, so remedial exercises for strengthening stomach muscles should be routinely incorporated into the warm-up program.

Any back pain that does not respond to rest and application of heat or cold, and certainly any recurrent lower back pain, should be checked by a physician experienced in sports injuries because of the tendency for persistent strains to develop into more serious conditions.

CONDITIONING EXERCISES

Exercises for Strengthening the Ankles

The gymnast who is recovering from an ankle sprain or fracture can begin recu-perating with nonweight bearing exercises that require the full range of the joint.

Exercise #1

1. Begin seated on the floor in a pike position, feet pointed.
2. Slowly begin flexing the feet at the ankle, maintaining the arch of the foot by grabbing and curling the toes under as the feet are pulled back as far as possible.
3. Release the toes, extending and stretching them out and away from each other. (This is done in the same manner as a cat stretching his paw.)
4. Maintaining the flexed position, emphasize the heel of the foot by feeling as though you are pressing the leg out and away from the hip socket, toward the opposite wall. Press the balls of the feet in the same manner and, finally, the toes. The foot is now pointed strongly through the tips of the toes, feeling a well stretched foot and arch, as the heel is contracted toward the calf of the leg.

Table 11.1 *Faulty Technique and Resulting Problems*

Faulty Technique	Resulting Problems
Faulty foot alignment due to forced turn-out (not initiating turn-out from hip).	Strain to the ligaments of knees and ankles.
Pressing big toe into floor or beam for balance.	Inflammation of the big toe joint. Disjointed toe—a condition in which the joint becomes dislocated with subsequent inflammation and broadening of the joint.
Clutching toes while foot is pointed to improve the appearance in the amount of arch in the foot.	Imbalance in the pulling of the two muscle groups which keep the toes extended, resulting in a loss of strength needed for strong propulsion.
a. Rolling inward of the foot (not maintaining the proper 3 point distribution of weight). b. Not returning heels firmly to floor following all movements of elevation, particularly those performed in a series.	Achilles tendon strain (tendinitis).
Inversion of the foot while in a pointed position (sickling in of the foot).	Overstretched lateral ligaments of the ankle, rendering them vulnerable to a sudden twisting or turning over (ankle sprain).
Overzealous pulling up of the thigh muscles or jamming of the patella in an effort to straighten the legs.	Pain just above or below the knee cap.
Poor use or development of the abdominal muscles.	Low back pain.
Leg limbering exercises performed before the body is sufficiently warmed up.	Pain in inner side of thigh near hip joint resulting from the extreme stretching of muscles without corresponding stretch to protect ligaments.
Pelvis tucked forward while leg is elevated and held in extended position to front or side (improper placement of pelvis).	Same as above.
Lack of conditioning exercises to strengthen hamstring group in back of thigh.	Hamstring strain resulting from an imbalance of the quadricep muscles in front of the leg and hamstring group behind the thigh.

Figure 11.1, 11.1a, 11.1b   *Conditioning exercise #1.*

Repeat this exercise several times smoothly and slowly.

Exercise #2

1. Begin lying on the back.
2. Bend the R. knee, placing the arms around the leg, hugging the knee and thigh into the chest.
3. Extend the L. leg straight up and to the ceiling (perpendicular to the floor.)

Figure 11.2, 11.2a, 11.2b   *Conditioning exercise #2.*

4. Bend the leg very slightly at the knee and flex the foot.
5. Turn the L. ankle inward and grab or curl the toes; then press the foot and and ankle as far outward as possible and flex open the toes. Repeat in this alternate fashion 8 times. Turn in and grab the toes . . . turn out and flex open.
6. Reverse the process so that the foot opens outward first, separating the toes, followed by the inward pull of the foot and ankle while flexing at the ankle and grabbing the toes. Foot opens outward and grabs, then inward and flexes. Repeat in this alternate fashion 8 times.

Repeat entire exercise on the right leg.

Exercises for Posterior Flexion of the Spine

These exercises are for stretching and strengthening the muscles of the back and, in general, to improve the posterior flexion of the spine.

Exercise #1:   Rock and roll:

1. Begin sitting on the floor, knees bent and close to chest, feet flat on floor, arms wrapped around legs, chin to chest.
2. Keeping the pelvis completely tucked and the abdominal muscles contracted, think of maintaining the same distance between the hip bones and the bottom of the ribs throughout the entire exercise.
3. Roll back and forth several times without stopping at any point until the exercise is completed. Be sure to roll evenly over each vertebrae, particularly in the lumbar region.

Exercise #2:   Rock and roll to plough:

1. Begin as in previous exercise.
2. As you roll back and onto the shoulders, begin to release the knees, extending over the head to the floor. Arms move down, palms on floor for support. Take a slow count of 4 to reach this position. Hold the position for a count of 4, relaxing the muscles of the spine, neck, and forehead while feeling the legs extending out from the back of the waist.
3. Slowly recover bringing knees to chest and return to beginning position.

Exercise #3:   Rock and roll to plough/variation:

1. Begin in straight seated position, palms on floor, hands beside hips.
2. Tuck hips under and contract abdominals to begin rolling backward, lifting both legs up straight as you do this. Continue rolling onto the shoulders, lifting the legs up and over the head to the plough position.
3. Roll through the spine allowing the legs to come with you, returning to the straight seated positon.

Repeat several times making sure to keep the abdominals well pulled in and the hips tucked.

Exercises for Strengthening the Lower Back and Waist

Exercise #1: Hip and leg extensions:

1. Begin lying on back, knees bent, feet slightly further than hip distance apart.
2. Bend R. knee to chest. Count 1.
3. Straighten R. leg, extending it to ceiling and lifting pelvis up. Count 2.
4. Keeping the R. leg straight, reach it out and down to the floor while pressing the pelvis still higher. Count 3-4.
5. Slide the L. foot along the floor to meet the R. (pelvis is still lifted and body is supported by shoulders and feet). Count 5-6.
6. Lower body to prone position by sliding feet out. Count 7-8.

Figure 11.3, 11.3a, 11.3b *Exercise for strengthening the back #1.*

Repeat several times with each leg.

Exercise #2:   Table top with leg extensions: This exercise is for strengthening the lower back, waist, and thighs.

1. Begin seated in pike position, hands on floor just behind hips. By support- ing the body with the hands, lift hips as high as possible, allowing the head to drop back as this is done. Legs remain straight.
2. Alternately lift and kick legs toward ceiling, endeavoring to maintain a tight body *without* dropping the hips and waist as the leg is lifted.

Repeat minimum of 8 kicks with each leg.

Figure 11.4, 11.4a *Exercise for strengthening the back #2.*

Exercise #3:   Arched torso developpés:

1. Begin lying on the back. Lift the chest, arching the back as high as possible, so that the torso is supported by the palms of the hand on the floor to the side of the body and also by the top of the head. Note that the chest must be stretched fully toward the ceiling and the shoulder blades must be con-

Figure 11.5, 11.5a, 11.5b   *Arched torso developpés (single leg).*

Figure 11.6, 11.6a *Arched torso developpés (double leg).*

tracted, while the palms of the hands firmly press into the floor to prevent strain on the neck and head.
2. Bring the R. knee toward the chest. Count 1.
3. Developpé the leg toward the ceiling. Count 2.
4. Lower the leg to the floor. Count 3-4.

Repeat 4 times with the right leg; 4 times with the left leg; 4 times with both legs together.

Exercises for Improving Poses Such as Arabesque and Attitude

Exercise #1:   The cobra/variation 1:   This exercise is for strengthening the upper and lower back. It also stretches the pectoral muscles and is helpful in improving posture (round shoulders) and the arabesque position.

1. Begin lying in a prone position on the stomach, hand on floor by the shoulders.
2. Begin lengthening the spine through the neck as you press down on the hands, lifting the chest off of the floor. Continue lifting the chest and arching as far as possible as you continue to feel a lengthening in the spine as though each vertebra was being pulled away from the other while the body arcs backward. Also feel the shoulder blades contract together and down toward the waist. At the height of the extension, feel the muscles along the back of the waist contract to help hold the arched position.

Figure 11.7 *Cobra exercise #1.*

3. Hold the position for a few seconds.
4. Slowly lower the body to the floor. As this is done, feel the front of the body being laid down on the floor like a tape measure. Keep the neck and head extended as long as possible, even as the bottom of the rib cage touches the floor. Finish lying in the prone position, face down. (As the body is lowered, try to support the body with the contraction of the back muscles, placing as little weight on the hands as possible.)

Repeat several times.

Exercise #2: Cobra/variation 2:

1. Begin lying on the floor in prone position, arms extended and beside the body.
2. Lift head, extending neck and spine as in previous exercise. Continue lifting as far as possible until the body is in a full arch position with the arms extended parallel to the floor. Note that there must be tension felt in the arms as the shoulder blades pull together and the arms pull back to aid in the lifting of the torso.
3. Hold the lifted position for several seconds.
4. Release the torso, lowering slowly to beginning position.

Repeat several times.

Figures 11.8 and 11.9 *Cobra exercise #2 (variation). Notice how clearly Michele shows the shoulder blades pulled down and the neck extended.*

Exercise #3: The crab/variation 1: This exercise is for strengthening the quadriceps, gluteals, hamstrings, lower back, and waist. It is also helpful for improving arabesque, attitude, and general control of the pelvis.

1. Lie in the prone position, face down, legs extended, heels together.
2. Bend the R. knee clasping the L. hand to the R. ankle.

3. Lift the foot as high as possible, stretching the R. thigh off the floor. Hold this position, feeling a contraction at the waist. Release after a slow count of 5.
4. Let go of the ankle without allowing the leg to drop (try to maintain the same position that the leg was previously in when held by the hand).
5. Slowly extend the arm and leg up toward the ceiling, continuing to feel the contraction in the waist.
6. Reach arm and leg in opposition, slowly lowering both to the floor. Be sure to feel the extension from the waist out through the finger tips and from the waist out through the toes as the body returns to the prone position.

Repeat several times, alternating sides.

Figure 11.10, 11.10a, 11.10b *Crab/Variation exercise #3.*

Exercise #4:   Variation 2–full crab:

1. Begin the exercise in the same manner as before.
2. Grasp each ankle and proceed through this exercise in the same manner as described in Crab Variation 1, but now using both legs at the same time.

Figure 11.11   *In this position the gymnast must feel the contraction of the muscles in the back of the waist.*

Figure 11.11a   *This position can only be held if the muscles in the back of the waist are engaged. The shoulder blades must be pulled down to the waist and the neck extended to prevent any tension in this area.*

Exercises for Strengthening the Abdominal Muscles

Exercise #1: This exercise strengthens lateral muscles (internal and external oblique).

1. Lie on the back, arms extended to sides, leg straight.
2. Slowly raise the R. leg to a vertical position.
3. Keeping both legs straight and shoulders firmly pressed into the floor, lower the R. leg to the floor, reaching toward the L. hand, while the head turns toward the right. (There should be a full twist in the waist as the ribs resist the pull of the reaching leg.)

4. Hold this position for a few seconds, feeling the stretch in the waist and hips.
5. Recover to the vertical position by first pessing the R. hip toward the left hand. Then, while maintaining this muscular pressure from the back of the hip, lift the leg to the ceiling. Both legs remain straight.
6. Lower leg to floor.

Repeat several times on each leg.

Exercise #2: This is another exercise to strengthen lateral muscles.

1. Lie on the back, arms extended at right-angles (T position), knees contracted to chest.
2. Maintaining both shoulders flat on floor, knees together, slowly lower the knees to the left side of body and to the floor (knees will be close to the

left elbow). Using the lateral muscles of the waist, feel a contraction of the muscles by firmly pressing the back of the ribs to the floor as the knees return to starting position.

Repeat 20 times, alternating side to side.

Exercise #3:   This exercise is for strengthening frontal abdominals.

1. Lie on the back, waist firmly pressed into floor, knees bent, and feet hip distance apart.
2. Continuing to firmly press the waist into the floor, bring the R. knee to the chest as you raise the head and shoulders just slightly off the floor. Hug the R. knee with the arms. As this is done, the L. leg will extend out and parallel to, but just slightly off, the floor. Hold this position for a few seconds. (The goal is to feel as though the body is resting on the back of the waist and pelvis, with the hip bones contracted up toward the waist, and the shoulders pulled firmly down lengthening the neck. As the L. leg extends, you will feel as though the extension began at the waistline.)

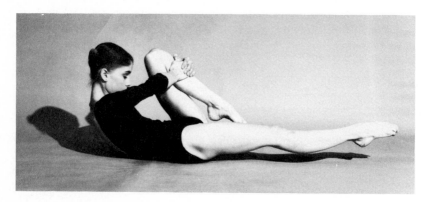

3. Change legs so that the R. leg is extended parallel to the floor and the L. knee is pulled to the chest. The change should be done as smoothly as possible so that the balance on the back of the waistline and pelvis is maintained with a tight contraction of the abdominals inward.

Repeat 10–20 times, alternating legs.

12

Presentation and Performance

For the gymnast, competition *is* the performance, and incorporated into the floor and beam routines must be all of the skills of the performer, as well as those of the athlete and the gymnast.

Presentation and performance is not an aspect of gymnastics that exists exclusively for competition. It must be integrated into the skills of the gymnast long before competition begins.

PRESENTATION AND PERFORMANCE SKILLS

The gymnast must combine elements of athletics and dance; consequently gymnastics walks a narrow line between a sport and a performing art. Which is it? It is both. More and more we see the barriers coming down as one area of endeavor recognizes the benefits of another. Football players study ballet; actors practice yoga and meditation; dance and dancers are becoming more athletic; athletes are becoming showmen; and books are written about the psychic side of sports, as everyone strives to use whatever tools are available to push toward greater achievement and understanding of a particular field.

The benefits of exposing the gymnast to some type of dance are obvious. The motivation is generally to improve dancing skills, enhance coordination, and lend grace to movement. The integration of dance and gymnastics needs to go beyond the training of a technician, however. Dance is a performing art and performance is the ultimate result of the training of a dancer. Regardless of whether or not the student ever makes that transition from class room to the stage, learning how to perform the movement and how to present oneself to the audience is essential. Performing is a skill in every sense of the word, it must be learned, and practiced in just the same manner as one practices tumbling and dance skills. It will not suddenly happen just because one is in front of the judges.

THE RESPONSIBILITY OF THE GYMNAST

The gymnast has a responsibility to both herself and to the movement. The tool is the body and there must be a full commitment to the dance movements each time they are performed. The body and the muscles must go through the steps many, many times to thoroughly integrate every aspect of the movement, the technique, the placement of the head, hands, torso, etc., and to make the movement as clear, precise, and effortless as possible. This will not happen if the gymnast marks through the steps or approximates the movements when practicing the routines. The steps must be danced full out each and every time, while fully integrating the gymnastic skills and the dance skills into one presentation. Encourage the gymnast to stop thinking of the routine as having the dance sections and the tumbling sections. As long as the two areas are segregated there will never be a complete and unified performance. Fulfilling the first responsibility means making a commitment to the dance movements in the same manner that the gymnast has committed to the most difficult tumbling skills. The gymnast knows not to half-heartedly go for a layout or full twist and should be encouraged to approach movement skills with that same commitment.

The gymnast's responsibilities to the coach are to concentrate fully in each workout session and to be receptive to constructive corrections. Always remember that criticism and corrections are positive input. It is through close observation, corrections, and refinement that the end product is improved. The gymnast must demonstrate a willingness to understand where problems exist in routines and then make a conscientious effort to correct them. Practice does not necessarily make perfect, only more automatic. Mistakes and errors can be practiced just as easily as perfection. The gymnast must learn to strive for perfection and this is accomplished through the constant application of corrections and adjustments. Finally, the gymnast must take the responsibility of remembering each correction and of working to improve the weak areas privately, between sessions with the coach. It does little good for the coach to spend the workout time reminding the gymnast of the same corrections given in the previous sessions. Not only is it self defeating, a tremendous waste of time, and an aggravation, but it hinders the progress of the gymnast by preventing the coach from moving on to new corrections or seeing where further adjustments might improve the routine.

The gymnast must have the courtesy to perform the movement to its fullest and in the manner in which it was given so that the coach can properly evaluate the quality and the structure of the routine or the movement. The coach should not have to use his/her imagination to determine this. If the gymnast does not perform movement full out, the coach cannot possibly know what her capabilities are, or whether the movements need adjustment.

Another responsibility of the gymnast to the coach is to remember that time is at a premium and one must always remain attentive. Since gymnastics is an individual endeavor and the coach must spend the greatest percentage of his/her time on a one-to-one basis, the gymnast must make the most of that time.

The final area of responsibility for the gymnast is to the audience. When the gymnast competes, her talent and skills are displayed to the judges and to the audience. The tool or instrument for that performance is the body and the manner of presentation. If the gymnast is going to present skill and talent to an audience there is an obligation to be worthy of their time and observation. Other artists display their talent or skills by virtue of something that they produce externally. The painter or sculptor, for example, displays his talent in the form of a design that the observer can view independent of the artist. Judgement of the artist's skills is through scrutiny of this external product. A rejection of the art work is not a rejection of the artist as a person, only as a craftsman. In any performing art there are sensitive egos involved and gymnastics is no different. The gymnast, like the dancer or the actor, presents skill and talent to be scrutinized in the form of a presentation through the physical body, the self, and the ego. Unfortunately, these cannot be separated; hence, just as the artist presents his sculpture, finished, polished, and ready for judgement, so must the gymnast be presented. Appearance must be neat, hair styled so as not to be distracting, and the performance must be free of distracting mannerisms, such as tugging on the leotard or tossing hair out of the face. The gymnast must come to the competition with confidence in her presentation and knowledge that she has perfected her routines to the best of her ability.

TAKING THE MOVEMENT BEYOND

"Taking the movement beyond." This is simply a matter of completing one movement before beginning the next. Never throw away a step or element before beginning the next. Each component is an important aspect of a larger one and there are no unimportant movements. Some steps may receive greater emphasis than others, some movements may be accented, and others may serve as connectors, but all are important. Always take a movement to its maximum position before going on to the next position. Otherwise it is like a series of unfinished thoughts or sentences. If the arms are to move out and then up, for example, be sure that they complete their outward movement before going up. If the foot and leg are brushing out and then up, make sure that the foot is fully stretched before the leg begins to move up.

ATTITUDE

The attitude of the gymnast is another area for consideration. In competition, no one cares if the gymnast is tired, angry, or has a headache. The fact that the gymnast has just fallen off of the beam ten minutes earlier, had an argument with a teammate, or recently learned that her father may be transferred to Alaska does not concern the judges or the audience. It is irrelevant to the performance and should not affect the presentation. The audience and the judges should be able to view and critique the gymnast's presentation and skills free from any sulking, glaring, or brooding on the part of the gymnast. There is an obligation to commit one's self fully to this end at every performance, whether in competition or during a workout session. It is not the responsibility of the judge or the coach to wade through extraneous issues that are irrelevant to her performance as a gymnast.

FACIAL EXPRESSION AND FOCUS

Using the face and the focus contributes to a more expressive performance and as with all other aspects of the performance, this, too, must be practiced. It is never too early to begin cultivating a pleasant expression or reminding the gymnast to direct the focus out instead of down. Telling the gymnast to smile during competition often seems artificial and almost inappropriate for the beam presentation, and forced smiles during workout sessions lack a certain relevancy. Therefore, developing a relaxed and pleasant expression will enhance the performance more than a routine filled with forced smiles.

Encourage the gymnast to direct her focus outward, actually seeing something and relating to it visually. With some gymnasts, their intensity is so great that they never lift their focus up at all; others seem to stare out into space almost as if in a trance. Of course they do this out of nervousness. It's like the small child who thinks that if he covers his eyes so that he can't see you, you can no longer see him. It is quite natural for the gymnast to feel conspicuous or alone and isolated during a presentation because, in fact, that is exactly the case. The practicing is over and the gymnast is truly alone. That moment of truth is familiar to all performing artists. Withdrawing only makes the observer uncomfortable and even more aware that that small figure in the distance is fearfully and tentatively making her way through the routine. By directing the focus out and making eye contact with objects about the room, the gymnast can present a more confident and direct approach, reflecting a sense of control over both the presentation and the routine. This sense of control is then automatically transmitted to the observers, making them more comfortable. As a result, the overall performance is dramatically improved.

The gymnast is frequently instructed by the coach to make eye contact with the judges, or to smile at the judges. This can be terribly difficult for the gymnast, particularly for the person who is not a natural performer. Obviously this is done to encourage the gymnast to perform the routine "to" the judge, since it is for their benefit that the competitor is there in the first place. However, making direct eye contact often makes the judge as uncomfortable as it does the gymnast. The idea of performing for the judges or the audience is certainly a valid aspect of competition, but it can be accomplished so much more easily and with the same effectiveness if the gymnast is instructed to focus just over the heads of the judges or the audience. In this way, they are included in the performance without any discomfort or embarrassment.

If the gymnast is encouraged to find enjoyment in the movement, to experience it rather than simply go through with it, to perform for pleasure, then this will automatically be reflected on the face. Teach selfishness in this regard. Performers are often seemingly inconsistent in their presentation—wanting to be received well, they try to perform for everyone else, never really enjoying the movement or the performance themselves. If only they would perform it for themselves first, thoroughly enjoying the experience and the movements, the audience would find it far more pleasurable and worthwhile as well.

THAT EXTRA MAGIC

That extra magic. Some performers have it, others do not. It is a psychic energy and it is not easily defined. Like any energy, it is an intangible form. You cannot see or feel it though the results are visually apparent in the presentation of the performer.

The magic of this energy can be observed when several performers are on stage, all dancing the same movements in the same manner, yet one individual seems to stand out above the others. Your eyes seem to be continually drawn to the performer with that extra something, that magic quality—a quality in the movement that appears when a dancer seems to hang suspended for an extra split second at the peak of a leap. Or the magic might be a kind of magnetism that extends out from the dancer and seems to envelop the surrounding space. It can be felt in the form of a kind of electricity that connects that performer to each individual in the audience. It is up to the performer to identify and tap this inner psychic force. This is not an external quality and therefore cannot be taught as a skill is taught. It is rather a personal vitality, a concept of being completely in touch with yourself and your surroundings.

Each individual must become aware of this energy within. When it is used, it can make the difference between mechanically going through the movements, or giving life and vitality to the performance. It is there for the gymnast to use. Help those you work with by encouraging them to find this power source buried within them. It will give them a keen sensitivity to their performance and an awareness of the space surrounding them.

Index

Page references in boldface are to major discussions of the topic.